SO-AAI-872

COLORADO FRONT RANGE SKI TOURS

ROCKY MOUNTAIN DIVISION
UNITED STATES SKI ASSN.

by TOM AND SANSE SUDDUTH

THE TOUCHSTONE PRESS
P.O. BOX 81
BEAVERTON, OREGON 97005

Library of Congress Catalog Card No. 75-27837
I.S.B.N. No. 0-911518-34-7

Maps courtesy of
U.S. Geological Survey

Copyright © 1975
by Tom and Sanse Sudduth

PREFACE

Eons ago, violent upheavals in the earth's surface lifted from beneath an inland sea the vast chain of the Rocky Mountains, a geological event so dramatic that it has been called the Laramide Revolution. Colorado's Front Range was formed during this era by a gradual folding of deep layers of granite rock, occasionally interrupted with high deposits of volcanic lava. For millions of years the Front Range has been sculptured by forces of erosion. Mountain rivers have cut deep canyons, glaciers have advanced, retreated, and advanced again, pushing earth into steep moraine ridges and carving high lakes. Today — in a single lifetime — these changes proceed imperceptibly. From the plains the towering peaks and deep saddles form an ever-constant horizon line, rugged and expansive and supremely beautiful.

Early settlers, however, looked on the Front Range not so much as a source of beauty but as a great barrier to transportation. The area first became known by the narrow passageways between high peaks: Rollins Pass, Arapaho Pass, Fall River Pass, Cameron Pass, all carried trappers and prospectors deeper into the mountains. Later railroad companies greatly expanded transportation within the Front Range. They laid tracks into silver-rich mining towns, then struggled to construct a line over the top of the Range itself. Evidence of this interesting past can be seen along some of the valleys and hillsides, even in wintertime. Old trailcuts appear along steep canyon walls, crumbling log cabins show above snow drifts, and rusted railroad tracks lie near abandoned mine shafts.

Despite all the intrusions of man however, the great expanse of wilderness still maintains its age-old integrity. Pine-covered slopes, glacial-carved lakebowls, and rocky mountaintops remain little changed from ten centuries ago. In winter, deep snows cover the roads and summer trails, creating many miles of easy-glide skiing. Creekbeds and valleys also become possible routes, leading through stark aspen groves and across snowy lakebeds. Cross-country climbs break above timberline to panoramic vistas, then open hillsides of unbroken snow permit long downhill returns. This back-country in winter is often silent and sometimes lonely but never empty. Mountain chickeedees and Gray jays flit from tree to tree, snowshoe hares stamp early morning tracks across the trail, and elk browse in the willow-filled meadows.

This book, then, invites the ski tourer to the Colorado Front Range, a land of varied geology, rich history, and unspoiled wilderness.

HOW TO USE THIS BOOK

The information capsule in boldface type reduce each tour to eight important facts, providing a means for quick comparison with other tours.

First, tours are divided into three categories: *half-day trip*, *one day trip*, and *overnight*. Two miles or less over easy terrain, the *half-day trip* gives a morning or afternoon of good exercise and fresh air. The *one day trip*, often stopping at a high mountain lake or an open park, takes the greater part of a day and requires a lunch stop. A destination point that puts the tourer too far into the backcountry to make safe return in the same day and necessitates a night of winter camping is called an *overnight*.

Next, tours are classified as *beginner*, *intermediate*, or *advanced* according to the tour length, elevation gain, and the distinctness of the trail. The *beginner* tour, short and below timberline, stays on flat and rolling terrain, often a wide, easily-discernible roadbed. A competent glide, step turn, and sidestep are usually needed for the small climbs and drops on an *intermediate* tour. Longer, sometimes inconspicuous, these trails require good endurance and a knowledge of map reading. The *advanced* tour varies in length but always requires good uphill technique for the steep climbs and accomplished step, snowplow, or telemark turns for the fast drops. Although the terrain on some overnight tours is gentle, these tours are all classified as advanced because of trail length and winter camping skills.

A major variable in tour difficulty is snow type: an hour of breaking trail in deep, wet snow can be harder than a day of gliding over unbreakable crust. A drop down a steep mountainside in powder snow can be easier than a run down a small hill of icy boiler plate. Thus, the tour classification will have to be adjusted accordingly.

Tour *distance* is measured one way only for tours that return over the same track. For circle tours the round trip distance is given. Steep switchback areas on cross-country trips are calculated as twice their linear distance. All distances are rounded to the nearest tenth of a mile; mileage signs in Rocky Mountain National Park, rounded to the nearest quarter of a mile, will not always agree with figures in this book.

Skiing time corresponds to one way or round trip distance. For beginner tours it is figured at 1-1½ miles per hour, a comfortable pace which allows time for rest stops, re-waxing, and picture taking. For intermediate and advanced tours skiing time is determined from a basic rate of 2 miles per hour and adjusted according to the steepness of the terrain. Lunch stops and driving time are not included.

Elevation gain, an important factor in determining tour difficulty and skiing time, measures the difference between the highest and lowest point on the tour.

Each life zone or elevation range holds unique rewards and hazards for ski touring as reviewed in SKI TOURING ALONG THE COLORADO FRONT RANGE (see below). The *maximum elevation* or highest point along the tour route is a useful indicator for these conditions.

Snowfall varies greatly from month to month and year to year in the Front Range. The *season* classification, however, offers the months when snow cover is most likely on a particular trail. This information represents the general consensus of Forest and Park Rangers and experienced ski tourers.

The last item in the information capsule is a listing of all appropriate *U.S.G.S. topographic maps* for the tour. These maps, available at most mountaineering shops, provide extremely useful information for ski touring, especially for the longer intermediate and advanced tours. Based on aerial photographs, they show the shape and elevation of the terrain, plot major trails, roads, creeks, and lakes, and differentiate between woodland, scrub, and open areas. With practice the tourer will be able to orientate himself when lost and to spot possible alternative routes.

Each ski tour description is organized into an introductory paragraph or two, a paragraph of driving directions, and several paragraphs of trail information. The introduction discusses prominent features of the tour such as interesting history and the origin of place names, spectacular viewpoints, outstanding ski runs, and prevalent hazards. The paragraph of driving directions provides instruction from the nearest major town, suggests a parking area, and notes variable conditions such as likely snow drifts and unplowed roads. The remaining paragraphs of trail information summarize the tour route. Good vistas, promising alternate routes, points of interest, and common tree types are included. Directions are based on true north rather than magnetic north and, except where a finer distinction is needed, they are rounded to eight points of the compass: N, NE, E, SE, S, SW, W, NW. Specific ski terms ("glide," "telemark," "sidestep," etc.) are used in the trail information not to prescribe touring technique but to provide a better understanding of the terrain. These terms are defined in the GLOSSARY.

The map printed in the book is an enlarged or reduced section of 7.5′ U.S.G.S. topographic maps used for the tour. Symbols that have been drafted onto the map such as "starting point," "avalanche danger," and "campsite" are listed in the LEGEND. The zig-zag line used for switchbacks is a symbol rather than a representation of the tour route.

SKI TOURING ALONG THE COLORADO FRONT RANGE

Creekbed trails at East Portal, steep climbs and drops in Rocky Mountain National Park, broad, rolling terrain near Red Feather Lakes — each area along the Front Range has its unique characteristics, each makes its distinctive demands on the tourer and offers special rewards. The general techniques of ski touring and winter camping are not discussed in this book. However, important points on ski touring in the Front Range are briefly noted.

WEATHER: The Front Range mountains, especially near the Continental Divide, tend to generate fast-changing, local weather systems independent of more general systems that may be dominating the area. Within a few minutes time, clouds can block the sun, temperatures can drop, and winds can increase, creating a wind chill of many degrees below zero. The tourer should prepare for these changes by always carrying an extra sweater and wind-proof outer garment.

Wind also builds unstable cornices on the leeward side of ridges and packs snow into hard, avalanche-prone slabs on steeper hillsides. After a period of new snow and wind, these areas should be avoided.

WAXING: Like snow, wax is crystaline in structure. It forms a bond with snow when the ski is motionless and weighted, creating grip; it releases the bond when the ski is moving and unweighted, allowing glide. The consistent snow conditions along the Front Range require the use of only two waxes for most of the winter — green wax for colder days, blue wax for warmer. Red wax is needed as the temperatures rise in March and April; klister is reserved for icy snow and slush.

LIFE ZONES AND ELEVATION RANGE: Snowfall is extremely variable along the Front Range. Near Boulder, for example, only a trace was recorded in February 1971 but a big 56.7 inches came in March. In the following year, however, 18.7 inches fell in February and only 11.5 inches were recorded for March. In general, March brings the most snowfall, followed by April, January, and February.

Snow cover, however, depends on more factors than the amount of snowfall. Exposure, slope, and elevation play extremely important roles. In the Montane Life Zone (8,000-10,000 feet) snow cover melts more quickly, staying longest along shaded, north-facing slopes. This area offers a better chance to see wildlife such as deer, elk, rabbits, and many species of birds. In the Sub-Alpine Life Zone (10,000-11,500 feet) snow cover is generally dependable from December through April on all hillsides. In spring, less wind and warmer days create ideal touring and camping conditions. Large snow banks remain through May and early June in the Alpine Life Zone (above 11,500 feet).

SPECIAL REGULATIONS

IN ROCKY MOUNTAIN NATIONAL PARK: On one day trips tourers are requested to sign the Trail Record at the trailheads, providing data for Park management.

On overnight trips, a written "Backcountry Use Permit" is required, obtained within one day of departure from the Park headquarters. All winter campers must carry stoves and enough fuel for all cooking and snow melting; wood fires are not permitted. Campsites must be in designated areas only and cutting of boughs for beds or lean-tos is prohibited. Dogs are not permitted in the Park.

EQUIPMENT

The sport of ski touring is easy, peaceful, and relaxing. It's the art of getting everything collected to go that always seems so complicated and frantic. This section is dedicated to the tourer who has driven in predawn hours to the trailhead and found everything except skis in his car, who has been ten miles into the backcountry and discovered that his huge lunch must still sit in the refrigerator. Here, then, is a handy, last-minute checklist of items for a day tour:

- SKIS, BOOTS, POLES
- HAT, GLOVES, WINDBREAKER,
   PARKA OR WOOL SWEATER
- WATER, LUNCH, EXTRA FOOD
- TOPO MAP AND COMPASS
- WAXES:
   Green
   Blue
   Red
   Klister
   Parafin
- SUN GLASSES AND SUN LOTION

- WATERPROOF MATCHES
- POCKET KNIFE
- AVALANCHE CORD
- FLASHLIGHT
- SPACE BLANKET
- SKI REPAIR KIT:
   Metal ski tip
   Binding parts (bail, cable, screws, etc.)
   Wire
   Adhesive tape
   Combination pliers/screwdriver
- FIRST AID KIT

AUTHORS' NOTE

We would like to express our gratitude to the many experienced ski tourers who contributed to the production of this guidebook. First, to those who traced their favorite trails on a topo map or actually guided us along the trail: in Boulder — John Whitbeck of Holubar Mountaineering LTD, Ingvar Sodal of Norsk LTD, Stan Nicholas of Frostline Outdoor Equipment, Gary Neptune of Neptune Mountaineering; in Allens Park — John Richards of Fawn Brook Inn; in Estes Park — Bill Evans of Rocky Mountain Ski Tours; in Fort Collins — Larry Moore of Wilderness Outfitter. An extra note of gratitude to Ann Leonard who guided us on many trails in Rocky Mountain National Park.

We also wish to thank the Rocky Mountain Division's Ski Touring Committee who initiated the project and provided financial assistance for the route-scouting. A special thanks to Bob McFetridge, Committee Chairman, who spent much voluntary time in following through with the original idea.

Several veteran ski tourers were hesitant to reveal their yet undiscovered trails. Like Colorado's early mountain men who kept an uneasy eye toward the onrush of "civilization," these people fear that the quiet and unspoiled winter wilderness, the final frontier, will soon be invaded by unthinking, insensitive crowds. We understand their concern but find only independent, ecologically-minded individuals among the newcomers. We remind everyone, however, to pack out all trash, build wood fires in designated sites only, and avoid cutting tree boughs for beds or lean-tos. Please leave nothing but your ski tracks!

All tours in this book were skied by the authors in the winter and spring of 1973-74. In an effort to make future editions of this book up-to-date and useful, we invite any comment, correction, or suggestion. Please send all material to the authors in care of: Colorado Ski Tours, Box 636, Steamboat Springs, Colorado 80477. Good touring!

LEGEND

STARTING POINT	●
TRAIL	— — — —
SWITCHBACK	⌐ -ᴧ⌐ →
ALTERNATE ROUTE	— →
MILEAGE	**9.0**
AVALANCHE DANGER	✳
CAMPSITE	▲

contents

area map

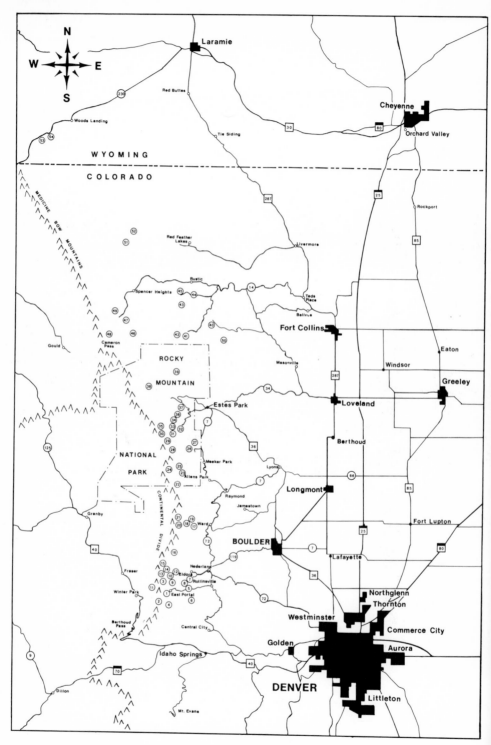

9

1 EAST PORTAL

Half-day trip
Classification: Beginner
Distance: 1.1 miles one way
Skiing time: ½-1 hour one way
Elevation gain: 400 feet
Maximum elevation: 9,600 feet
Season: Mid-December through March
Topographic map:
  U.S.G.S. East Portal, Colo. 7.5′

The short, easy climb from the east portal of historic Moffat Tunnel to the spacious clearing where Rogers Pass and Heart Lakes trail and Forest Lakes trail divide is an ideal tour for beginners, families, and late starters. The stopping point and good lunch spot, if not windy, offers a view of the snowcapped Continental Divide, several interesting log cabins for investigation, and a gentle slope for downhill skiing. Following South Boulder Creek southwest the private property access road is restricted to "foot travelers only," eliminating competition between tourers and snowmobilers. Occassional high winds plus heavy trail use on December, January and February week-ends can cause rough, packed snow; midweek and early spring touring is recommended.

Equally as interesting as the scenic attractions is the massive concrete portal of Moffat Tunnel at the tour's beginning. David Moffat, a miner, banker and railroader, had been an early advocate of a railroad passage west through the Rockies and he invested millions toward the realization of this grandiose idea. However not until 1928, 17 years after Moffat's death, did the tunnel carry the first train under the Continental Divide.

Drive on Colorado 72 or 119 to Rollinsville. Turn west onto the dirt road and proceed 8.2 miles through Tolland to East Portal. Out-of-the-way parking is available for many cars on the north side of the road near the tunnel.

Pack skis across the railroad tracks and aqueduct via an access road 50 yards east of the portal; cross through a heavy metal pipe gate, and begin skiing southwest across 200 yards of open area to a barbed wire fence. The trail can be windy around this open tunnel area but is more protected in the trees just beyond the fence. Rather than opening the gate or crawling through the wires, pass between the gate and gatepost tree.

Ski southwest into the trees either cross-country or over the summer road, keeping above and to the right of South Boulder Creek. Wind past several private cabins; continue in and out of trees to a large meadow at 0.5 mile where Arapaho Creek joins South Boulder Creek. In the spring this creek cascades down the steep hillside under the snow, filling the meadow with a reverberating drum-like sound. The little hillside to the right makes a good slope for beginning downhill practice.

Re-enter the trees on the roadbed and climb gradually 60 feet above the creek bottom. Ski through another small meadow to a spacious clearing marked in the middle with a gravesite and trail sign.

The tour can be continued southwest to Rogers Pass and Heart Lakes (No. 2) or northeast to Forest Lakes (No. 3).

East Portal of Moffat Tunnel

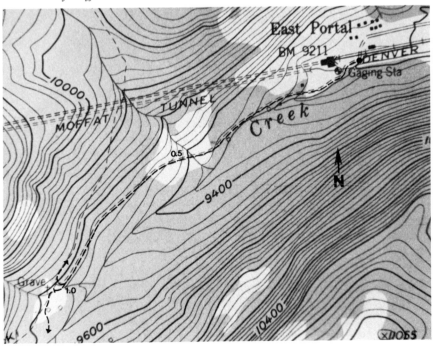

2 ROGERS PASS AND HEART LAKES

One day trip
Classification: Advanced
Distance: 6.8 miles round trip
Skiing time: 3-5 hours round trip
Elevation gain: 2,100 feet
Maximum elevation: 11,300 feet
Season: December through April
Topographic maps:
  U.S.G.S. East Portal, Colo. 7.5'
  U.S.G.S. Empire, Colo. 7.5'

Spruce and fir trees shelter the steady cross-country climb along South Boulder Creek almost the entire way but in the last 0.2 mile to Rogers Pass Lake the trees give way to a dramatic panoramic view. Expansive bowls in the 12,000 foot mountain range west cut a scalloped horizon line into the sky and cradle the timberline Rogers Pass and Heart Lakes. Viewed from Rogers Pass Lake, Haystack Mountain to the south shows only its triangular granite face but from Heart Lake its unique flat top and steep sides are visible.

Wind and snow storms at 11,000 feet are severe and the tourer should remain alert for early signs of bad weather. Also beware of potential avalanche danger on the steep mountainside southeast of Rogers Pass Lake. In spring, wear glacier goggles for protection against snow reflection. On the return loop the fast drop from Heart Lake through the forested hillside to South Boulder Creek requires competent telemark and step turns. This exhilerating run plus the tour's high elevation determine the advanced classification. For an easier, slightly longer tour eliminate the loop and return down the South Boulder Creek trail.

Drive on Colorado 72 or 119 to Rollinsville. Turn west onto the dirt road and proceed 8.2 miles through Tolland to East Portal. Out-of-the-way parking is available for many cars on the north side of the road near the tunnel.

Pack skis across the railroad tracks and aqueduct; cross through a heavy metal pipe gate, and begin skiing southwest across 200 yards of open area to a barbed wire fence. Pass between the gate and gatepost tree and head southwest into the trees, keeping above and to the right of South Boulder Creek. Wind past several private cabins and through a large meadow where Arapaho Creek joins South Boulder Creek. Re-enter the trees on the roadbed; climb gradually 60 feet above the creek bottom; continue to a spacious clearing, marked in the middle with a gravesite and trail sign.

Cross to the southwest end of the clearing past two log buildings. Enter the trees either immediately north of the creekbed on a red-flagged cross-country route or, if heavy snow has obscured the trail, on the clearer but steeper South Boulder Creek summer trail higher up the hillside. After 0.2 mile the flagged route joins the summer trail.

Climb southwest up several steep sections. Bend south near the 2.0 mile mark when the trail levels. As the summer trail becomes increasingly more difficult to find, ski cross-country on either side of the creekbed. Begin turning west, curving with the snow-covered mountain range to the south. Traverse a steep section out of the loosely-spaced trees into a flat meadow. Stop for lunch in the trees if weather protection is needed.

Continue west to the east lip of Rogers Pass Lake then turn north and make the last 200 foot climb to the broad, high mesa east of Heart Lake. Begin the return loop northeast across the mesa to the Heart Lake drainage and drop gradually 0.3 mile to denser trees. The small, green East Portal buildings 3.0 miles away can be seen just before entering the trees. Drop more steeply through the trees, staying close to creekbed until intercepting the South Boulder Creek trail. Follow the ski tracks out or for more challenge return down the South Boulder creekbed itself.

Gravesite at fork to Heart and Rogers Pass Lakes

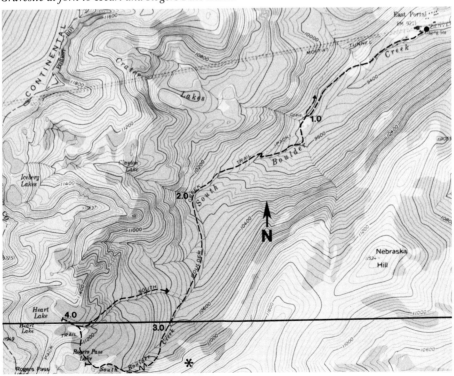

3 FOREST LAKES

One day trip
Classification: Intermediate
Distance: 3.5 miles one way
Skiing time: 2½-3 hours one way
Elevation gain: 1,640 feet
Maximum elevation: 10,840 feet
Season: December through April
Topographic map:
   U.S.G.S. East Portal, Colo. 7.5'

A southern, lower cirque with avalanche chutes between granite outcroppings and a nothern, higher cirque with smooth, white sides and a corniced top form the west wall of a larger amphitheater surrounding upper Forest Lake. The Boulder Group of the Colorado Mountain Club has flagged the trail to this spectacular scenery as part of an annual Cross Country-Alpine Forest Lakes ski race and a tourer can follow the race course itself for the full 2,000 foot climb and 6.0 mile length. The recommended tour, however, eliminates the weather-exposed ridge and 400 feet of elevation.

With deep powder or icy snow the tour can challenge the advanced skier but usually the intermediate skier with correct wax and with plenty of time will have no problem. Pack in drinking water during midwinter months.

Drive on Colorado 72 or 119 to Rollinsville. Turn west onto the dirt road and proceed 8.2 miles through Tolland to East Portal. Out-of-the-way parking is available for many cars on the north side of the road near the tunnel.

Pack skis across the railroad tracks and aqueduct; cross through a heavy metal pipe gate, and begin skiing southwest across 200 yards of open area to a barbed wire fence. Pass between the gate and gatepost tree and head southwest into the trees, keeping above and to the right of South Boulder Creek. Wind past several private cabins and through a large meadow where Arapaho Creek joins South Boulder Creek. Re-enter the trees on the roadbed; climb gradually 60 feet above the creek bottom; continue to a spacious clearing, marked in the middle with a gravesite and trail sign.

Climb to the top of the clearing and turn northeast on a roadcut, a steep climb at first but soon more gradual. A break in the trees on the east reveals the green East Portal buildings on the valley floor and forested, snow-capped Nebraska Hill to the south. Dip across Arapaho Creek near the 1.5 mile mark then climb sharply and begin curving north then northwest on the road. The white mountain dome south of Arapaho Lakes soon dominates the view west. Stay to the right of Arapaho Creek but don't turn east on the flagged uphill leg of the race course. Ski northwest nearly 1.0 mile either cross-country through the many little meadows or on the wide, straight electric-line swath through the trees to the flat, junction meadow of Arapaho and Forest Lakes creeks. With a view of the dome-shaped mountain south of Arapaho Lakes and the sharper peak farther north the meadow makes a good rest and lunch spot.

Turn north and traverse the hillside west of Forest Lakes creek on the flagged route. Near the top ski the steep-banked creekbed itself to lower Forest Lake. Climb the small hill on the northwest side of the lake, then cross through the final snow fields to upper Forest Lake. Return cross-country down the easy, rolling drops and through the scattered trees. For the thrill-seeker, the steep part of the Forest Lakes creekbed makes a roller-coaster drop to the flat meadow below.

14

Cirque above Forest Lakes

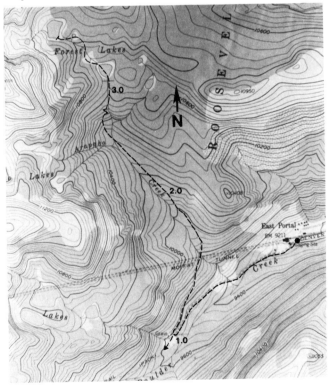

4 MAMMOTH GULCH

One day trip
Classification: Beginner to Intermediate
Distance: 5.0 miles one way
Skiing time: 3-3½ hours one way
Elevation gain: 1,420 feet
Maximum elevation: 10,340 feet
Season: January through March
Topographic maps:
  U.S.G.S. Nederland, Colo. 7.5'
  U.S.G.S. Central City, Colo. 7.5'
  U.S.G.S. Empire, Colo. 7.5'

In the first open half mile the Mammoth Gulch Road gains an excellent overlook of Tolland and expansive South Boulder Park. Today a quiet huddle of weathered buildings, Tolland served during the first quarter of this century as a bustling tourist resort along the Moffat Railroad. A souvenir shop, picnic shelter, and lunchrooms in the picturesque mountain village accommodated hundreds of sightseers that arrived each summer day for an outing in nearby Medicine Bow Forest. A winter outing in the same rolling hills, now part of the Roosevelt National Forest, still makes a memorable day for the ski tourer.

The tour route follows the conspicuous Mammoth Gulch Road on a steady climb up open Baltimore Ridge. Rusted mining equipment and tumbled mine shacks farther down the road give clues to Mammoth Gulch history. On days without wind, the open gulch bottom provides an alternate return route.

Drive on Colorado 72 or 119 to Rollinsville; turn west onto the dirt road and proceed to the small mountain village of Tolland. Turn south 0.2 mile west of Tolland onto the Mammoth Gulch Road and continue as far as road conditions permit. Park off the road.

Begin skiing southwest on the wide road to a lookout of flat Boulder Park and the mountain range west. White roadcuts terrace the mountainside, a series of old Moffat Railroad switchbacks called Giants Ladder. This first section of road often has crusty or drifted snow but snow conditions improve considerably in the aspen and pine. Climb steadily on the winding road, soon passing the smooth snow patch of Teller Lake in the gulch bottom.

Continue on the level, middle Mammoth Gulch Road as the Mammoth Basin Road climbs southeast and the Nebraska Hill Route drops southwest.

Glide through more widely scattered aspens and conifers and soon break from the trees onto a large, open mountainside. A flattened gulch bottom west marks the general area of snow-covered Mammoth Creek Reservoir; above the road east are several old mine-pits. Cross the scrubby mountainside, contour west, and head back into the trees along the steep north side of Pile Hill.

The road passes a rusted, cylindrical steam boiler and tumble-down log shack, then continues the steady climb through thick timber up the hillside, passing an abandoned road-grader. The road ends at the private Mammoth Mining Company buildings. Ski back to the less-dense timber near the steam boiler, and glide down the hillside to the Mammoth Gulch bottom. Return down the gulch; pass flat Mammoth Creek Reservoir, and follow a roadbed back to the Mammoth Gulch Road.

Mammoth Gulch Road

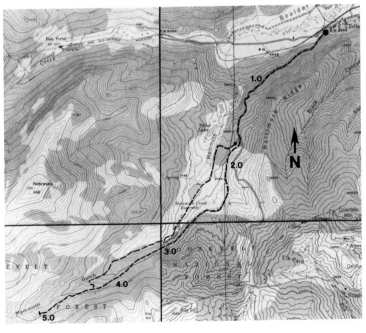

5 JENNY CREEK

Half-day trip
Classification: Beginner
Distance: 2.1 miles one way
Skiing time: 1-1½ hours one way
Elevation gain: 440 feet
Maximum elevation: 9,320 feet
Season: January through March
Topographic map:
    U.S.G.S. Nederland, Colo. 7.5'

#5 JENNY CREEK

Due to excessive use, access across privately-owned land from Tolland north into Jenny Creek has recently been closed to the ski touring public. Please respect this closure! A tentative right-of-way across private land from Jenny Creek west to the Roosevelt National Forest is currently available from the Lake Eldora Ski Area, provided by courtesy of the Henry Toll Ranch and the Lake Eldora Corporation. See page 22 for further information.

On busy winter weekends the Lake Eldora Ski Area often becomes crowded with ski tourers heading to the Jenny Creek area. A more convenient, uncrowded route to this area is from Tolland. The maze-like tour beginning crosses through several gates, railroad tracks, and a viaduct in windswept Boulder Park, then leads to a secluded, north-facing slope where beautiful blue spruce shade the trail. Then the tour route crosses Jenny Creek three times in a few hundred yards on decaying log bridges. A branch trail forks immediately north of a snow-covered pond and intercepts the Moffat Road farther west. On warm, spring days touring can be exceptional on this high road.

Drive on Colorado 72 or 119 to Rollinsville. Turn west onto the Tolland road, and proceed 4.8 miles to the intersection of a branch road which crosses the railroad tracks north. A parking space along the south side of the Tolland road is usually clear of snow.

Follow the branch road north into Boulder Park; cross through a gate, and proceed through a windswept open area. Cross through two metal gates on either side of the railroad tracks; angle right and continue across a viaduct. Enter the trees near an electric line and glide north on the road. Wind reduces the snow depth in Boulder Park but conditions improve considerably in the sheltering trees.

Climb through a gate and begin a gradual climb, turning right up the hill when a road forks left. Ski through a clearing filled with sawmill slabs and a junk car, pass through a barbed wire fence, and take the northwest trail fork toward Jenny Creek. Curve north into a shady glen of deep snow. Double pole to creek level and weave west up the drainage, crossing Jenny Creek three times over crumbling log bridges. Break out of the trees and come to a snow-covered pond immediately west of the trail. Blue spruce, also called water spruce due to their creek and pond habitat, shade much of the trail.

Ski northwest on the main trail; pass east of the pond and continue straight where a trail forks west. The branch trail crosses Jenny Creek and intercepts the Moffat Road which switchbacks to the ridgetop. Wind north on the Jenny Creek trail, pass a fork west along Antelope Creek (No. 8), and continue through a large meadow area to the east-west trail to Yankee Doodle Lake (No. 9) and Guinn Mountain (No. 10). The meadow makes a nice stopping point and picnic spot.

18

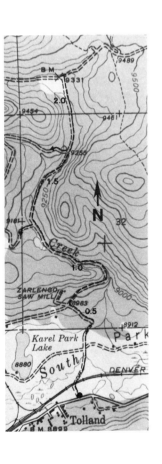

In Jenny Creek meadow

6 JENNY LIND GULCH

Half-day trip
Classification: Beginner to Intermediate
Distance: 2.0 miles one way
Skiing time: 1-1½ hours one way
Elevation gain: 1,050 feet
Maximum elevation: 9,850 feet
Season: Mid-December through March
Topographic map:
  U.S.G.S. Nederland, Colo. 7.5′

In 1850, Swedish opera singer Mme. Jenny Lind, "the greatest musical wonder in the world," made a triumphant singing tour in the United States. The Swedish Nightingale gained such widespread popularity that it is not surprising to find a Jenny Lind Gulch in her honor.

On winter weekends when trails around the East Portal and Eldora areas are busy with tourers, often only a snowshoe rabbit or two have left tracks on the trail up nearby Jenny Lind Gulch. It is an easy tour through a climax stand of giant ponderosa pine and englemann spruce and across several icy brooks to a hillside playground covered with scattered pine.

Drive on Colorado 72 or 119 to Rollinsville. Turn west and proceed 4.0 miles on the Tolland/East Portal road; stop 1.5 miles before Tolland at the jeep road leading south up Jenny Lind Gulch. This inconspicuous starting point is 0.1 mile past a north road fork across the railroad tracks and creek. Park off the road on the south side.

Ski around the barbed wire gate and head south on the jeep road through a meadow with tall ponderosa pine. Fork right when the left fork turns up through a private gate; follow the willow-filled creek on the east side, then at 0.4 mile cross to the west side. The gulch bottom gradually separates east and down as the trail, near the treeline, traverses the mountainside. Barren Jumbo Mountain, crisscrossed with mining roads, can be seen east from the clearings.

Cross a creek unmarked on the 1942 topo and make an easy climb through giant spruce and pine trees. At 1.0 mile, after a tricky creek crossing over a dilapidated log bridge, enter the trees again and weave through pine seedlings in the middle of the road. Climb more steeply up the mountainside; pass through an intersecting drainage and continue up a narrowing roadcut. No turnouts plus lodgepole branches across the road here add excitement to the downhill return. Gradually ski out of the trees and traverse the open mountainside. Switchback west to the top for good downhill skiing through the scattered pine. For a longer tour follow the drainage southwest, cross the gulch to the east fork, and explore the mining roads. Return over the ski tracks.

Snow Shower on trail

Access across privately-owned land in Jenny Lind Gulch has recently been closed to the ski touring public. Please respect this closure! Additional areas within the Boulder-Estes Park Forest Service District open to ski tourers include the South St. Vrain Trail (parking available along the Beaver Reservoir Road), the Coney Flats Trail north and west from Beaver Reservoir (also used by snowmobiles), the Middle St. Vrain and Rock Creek area above Allenspark, and the North Fork of the Big Thompson (access either via a right-of-way from Glen Haven or via the trailhead in Dunraven Gulch). For more details on these areas, contact the Boulder-Estes Park Districts, 2995 Baseline — Room 16, Boulder, CO 80303.

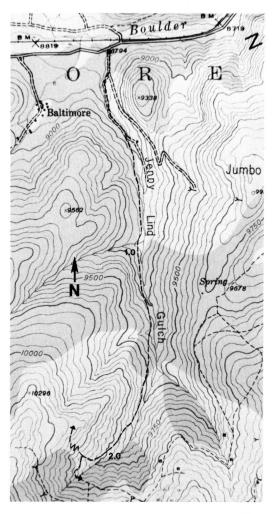

7 PETERSON LAKE AND LAKE ELDORA

Half-day trip
Classification: Beginner
Distance: 1.4 miles one way
Skiing time: ½-1 hour one way
Elevation gain: 380 feet
Maximum elevation: 9,610 feet
Season: Mid-December through March
Topographic map:
U.S.G.S. Nederland, Colo. 7.5′

Chimney ruin near Lake Eldora

Near Lake Eldora Ski Area a myriad of trails, each crowded with tourers on midwinter weekends, crisscross the flat meadows and wind up and down the creek drainages. Beginning from the east end of Peterson Lake this short, pleasant tour passes west of Lake Eldora and climbs and drops through sheltering lodgepole to a crossroads. From this point well-traveled paths invite exploration farther west (No's. 8, 9 & 10) and lead north and south looping back to the main trail.

Drive on Colorado 119 southwest of Nederland; turn north at a sign marking the route to Lake Eldora Ski Area. Curve southwest to the Middle Boulder Creek valley floor and fork left at 1.5 miles onto the ski area access road. Tire chains or snow tires are often required for this road after snowstorms or windstorms. Continue up Tennessee Mountain to the east end of Peterson Lake. Plowed parking for six to ten cars usually is kept open on the north side of the road.

Cross to an old jeep road on the south side of the ski area road and begin climbing southwest through the few aspen and fir trees. A prominent limber pine, gnarled and lightning-scarred, weathers the storms on the exposed hillside near the start. Swing south past an old log cabin on the right and continue the curve into a clearing with two newer cabins. Interesting brick and stone chimneys and fire-blackened trees are evidence of a fire.

From the clearing glide south across the west end of Lake Eldora and a small pond. Angle slightly right from the drainage and climb gradually on a sheltered jeep road into the trees. Turn right again where a cable crosses the road and follow the red flags on the lodgepole-hemmed trail up then down the hillside. At times the open marsh area is visible southwest through the trees. Continue southwest across the end of the open marsh area; make a gradual climb up a long hill. The few turnouts and iced snow from heavy trail use increase the difficulty of this hill on the return route. At the top a break in the trees shows the ski runs of Lake Eldora Ski Area.

Double pole west down a long, easy drop on the narrow trail, watching for oncoming tourers. Continue west across the level terrain passing the old University of Colorado practice track which merges on the left; come to a trail crossroads 0.1 mile farther. Straight ahead the trail drops to Jenny Creek. The practice track continues on the south fork curving left and returning to the crossroads. The north fork makes a short climb to a vista, then drops east of the ski area to the ski area road. From the road drop to Peterson Lake and return east to the parking area.

#7 PATTERSON LAKE AND LAKE ELDORA

In 1975-76 the Lake Eldora Ski Area opened an exciting, carefully-planned ski touring trail system on the privately-owned land around Lake Eldora. The touring trailhead, located east of Ho-Hum Lift at the far east end of the ski area, leads to fifteen or more interlinked trails, each identified by sign and difficulty classification. A trail pass, $2.00 Adult/$1.00 Child, may be purchased at the trailhead. No dogs, hikers, snowshoers, or snowmobilers are allowed on the ski trails.

Public access, free of charge, is now provided from the Lake Eldora Ski Area to Roosevelt National Forest. Free parking is available in the lower ski area parking lot for tourers using the public access. A one-way lift ticket to the top of the ski area mountain is not offered at this time. For current information on ski touring facilities, policies, and snow conditions, contact: Lake Eldora Corporation, P.O. Box 438, Nederland, CO 80466. Call: (303) 447-8012.

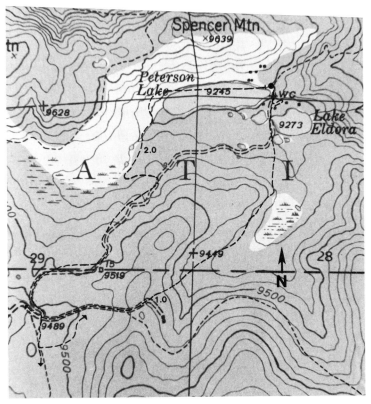

8 ANTELOPE CREEK

One day trip
Classification: Intermediate to Advanced
Distance: 6.7 miles round trip
Skiing time: 4½-5 hours round trip
Elevation gain: 420 feet
Maximum elevation: 9,610 feet
Season: Mid-December through March
Topographic map:
 U.S.G.S. Nederland, Colo. 7.5′

From 1904 to 1929 steam locomotives of the Denver, Northwestern & Pacific Railway crossed a large clearing near Antelope Creek on the first rung of "Giant's Ladder," then looped back through Tunnel 31 and continued the arduous climb over Rollins Pass. Today a protruding mound of earth on the north hillside of the clearing identifies the old roadbed and a large pit and steel beam at the northwest end mark the southern portal of collapsed Tunnel 31.

Drive on Colorado 119 southwest of Nederland; turn north onto the Eldora road and after 1.5 miles fork left toward Lake Eldora Ski Area. Continue up Tennessee Mountain to the east end of Peterson Lake. Parking space for several cars is usually kept open on the north side of the road.

Cross to the south side of the ski area road and begin climbing southwest on an old jeep road, soon curving northeast to a fire-burned clearing with stone and brick chimney ruins. Glide south across the west end of Lake Eldora and a small pond, then angle right on the road into the trees. Turn right where a cable crosses the road and follow the red flags up then down the hillside. Cross the southwest end of an open, marshy area; climb another hillside through blazed lodgepole pine. Double pole west down the hillside and continue across level terrain to a crossroads.

For an intermediate route head west, descending the hill and making a quick left turn to Jenny Creek meadow. Turn south at the meadow and follow Jenny Creek into the trees. For an advanced route ski south from the crossroads, staying right where the old University of Colorado practice track loops left; after 0.4 mile come to a clearing with high stumps at the west end. Cross the clearing southwest, then snowplow the steep hillside, crossing the drainage with a quick drop and step turn left. Join the intermediate route at the hill bottom; ski into the trees and across a meadow, staying between the steep mountainside east and Jenny Creek west.

Cross a willow-filled meadow, continuing through trees on the east mountainside and eventually curving south-southeast and climbing slightly. As the trees break to another large open area turn southwest and cross Jenny Creek, staying north of the merging drainage. The snow-filled roadbed, sheltered by lodgepole pine, climbs northwest and north away from the drainage, then bends again northwest and continues to a large clearing. In this clearing a bit of railroad history can be reconstructed from the old log structures, mounds of earth, and large pits.

Continue to the northwest end of the clearing. Climb left of a large pit through lodgepole pine, passing another pit; turn west-northwest onto the south side of Antelope Creek drainage and glide along the old roadbed through fir and englemann spruce to the creek. One trail continues south up Antelope Creek and another forks west 1.2 miles to Jenny Creek, both offering alternative routes for the adventurous tourer. Continue east across a meadow to a steep mountainside, crossing the inconspicuous Jenny Creek drainage and completing the loop. Turn north and return via the intermediate route.

24

Mine ruins above Antelope Creek

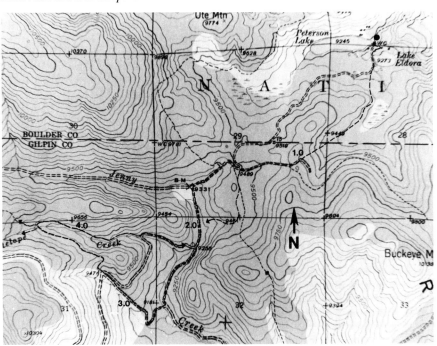

9 YANKEE DOODLE LAKE

One day trip
Classification: Intermediate to Advanced
Distance: 5.7 miles one way
Skiing time: 4-4½ hours one way
Elevation gain: 1,490 feet
Maximum Elevation: 10,720 feet
Season: Mid-December through March
Topographic maps:
  U.S.G.S. Nederland, Colo. 7.5′
  U.S.G.S. East Portal, Colo. 7.5′

Yankee Doodle Lake, neatly tucked in the crook of a rocky, cane-shaped range, was the most advertised scenic spot along the old railroad route over Rollins Pass. A mound of earth tailings on the north side of the lake, faintly discernable under deep snow cover, still remain from an 1879-1880 effort of David Moffat to construct a 2,000 foot tunnel under the range. A clear route to Yankee Doodle Lake winds through tall lodgepole pine, englemann spruce and silver-hued blue spruce

along Jenny Creek, then dissipates during the last mile to a cross-country climb. Find a lunch spot in the protective trees well below the windy bowl area around the lake. A two-car loop tour from Peterson Lake to East Portal links the Yankee Doodle Lake tour with the Forest Lakes tour (No. 3). Swing south one-half mile before Yankee Doodle Lake and bridge the range between Jenny Creek and Forest Lakes.

Drive on Colorado 119 southwest of Nederland; turn north onto the Eldora road and after 1.5 miles fork left toward Lake Eldora Ski Area. Continue up Tennessee Mountain to the east end of Peterson Lake. Parking space for several cars is usually kept open on the north side of the road.

Cross to the south side of the ski area road and begin skiing southwest on an old jeep road, soon curving northeast to a fire-burned clearing with stone and brick chimney ruins. Glide south across the west end of Lake Eldora and a small pond, then angle right on the road into the trees. Turn right where a cable crosses the road and follow the red flags up then down the hillside. Cross the southwest end of an open, marshy area; climb another hillside through blazed lodgepole pine and ski across level terrain to a crossroads.

Shuss west down the hillside, maneuvering a quick left turn. The flat run-out of Jenny Creek meadow allows a fast downhill run when the trail has cleared of returning tourers. Glide west along the north side of the meadow, then follow the trail north of Jenny Creek through the englemann and blue spruce. Continue in and out of the trees; near the 3.0 mile mark cross the willow-filled meadow of an inconspicuous branch creek. Begin climbing above Jenny Creek but keep left where a branch trail climbs more steeply to Guinn Mountain (No. 10). Soon the bald mountaintop south across the valley, cut by the high Moffat Road, becomes a prominent landmark.

Swing southwest after the creekbed rises again to the trail and pass a roadbed that returns east along the south side of Jenny Creek. When the trail disappears at the flat creek drainage, cross-country west through limber pine. A red-flagged route hugs the steep side of Guinn Mountain for a short ways, then winds back to Jenny Creek.

Turn northwest, then gradually north, and make the steady climb staying on the right side of Jenny Creek. Cross windswept Moffat Road and drop into the white bowl of Yankee Doodle Lake. Return over the ski tracks.

Above Yankee Doodle Lake

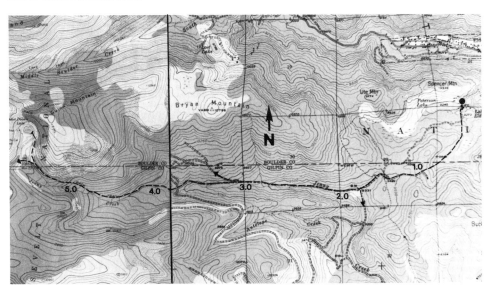

10 GUINN MOUNTAIN

One day trip
Classification: Advanced
Distance: 5.2 miles one way
Skiing time: 3½-4 hours one way
Elevation gain: 1,850 feet
Maximum elevation: 11,080 feet
Season: Mid-December through March
Topographic Maps:
    U.S.G.S. Nederland, Colo. 7.5′
    U.S.G.S. East Portal, Colo. 7.5′

An aerie perched near the mountaintop, the Guinn Mountain Hut provides the ski tourer with cozy refuge from bitter wintry storms. The Colorado Mountain Club maintains the hut and asks any visitor to share with the housekeeping duties. Easy gliding from Peterson Lake to Jenny Creek allows a gradual warm-up for the steeper climb to the hut. After the many weekend tourers have packed the trail, the huffing-puffing two hour climb *up* Guinn Mountain is surpassed in difficulty only by the heart-thumping half hour descent *down* Guinn Mountain.

Drive on Colorado 119 southwest of Nederland; turn north onto the Eldora road and after 1.5 miles fork left toward Lake Eldora Ski Area. Continue up Tennessee Mountain to the east end of Peterson Lake. Parking space for several cars is usually kept open on the north side of the road.

From the south side of the ski area road begin skiing southwest on a drifted jeep trail, soon curving northeast to a fire-burned clearing with stone and brick chimney ruins. Glide south across the west end of Lake Eldora and a small pond, then angle right on the road into the trees. Turn right where a cable crosses the road and follow the red flags up then down the hillside. Cross the southwest end of an open, marshy area; climb another hillside through blazed lodgepole pine and ski across level terrain to a crossroads.

From the crossroads ski west down the hill to Jenny Creek meadow, shussing into the flat run-out at the hill bottom. Follow the road on the north side of the large meadow and continue west into the trees, staying north of Jenny Creek. Tall blue spruce, some with a very silvery hue, decorate the creek drainage. Wind through several small meadows, cross an inconspicuous branch creek near the 3.0 mile mark, and begin climbing gradually above Jenny Creek.

Turn right as the trail forks to Yankee Doodle Lake (No. 9); begin climbing more steeply up the Guinn mountainside. Cross-country west over the rising and falling mountainside, following the red-flagged trail. Scattered limber pine, indicating entrance into the high sub-alpine life zone, open to reveal the Jenny Creekbed far down the mountainside. Three bald mountains protrude from the forested hillside south and snow-capped peaks near Forest Lakes glisten on the horizon farther west.

Resume the climb into a drainage filled with towering englemann spruce. Follow the drainage as it widens to a large ravine, soon passing an old log cabin. Switchback west above the ravine floor and follow the well-flagged trail southwest and west through the trees. Break into a long, east-west meadow and continue another few hundred feet to the Guinn Mountain Hut on the south side. Return over the ski tracks.

Cabin ruin on Guinn Mountain

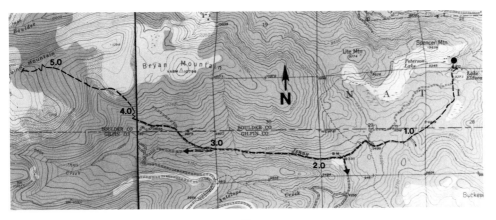

11 ROLLINS PASS

Overnight
Classification: Advanced
Distance: 17.6 miles one way
Skiing time: 9½-12 hours one way
Elevation gain: 2,430 feet
Maximum elevation: 11,660 feet
Season: Mid-December through March
Topographic maps:
   U.S.G.S. Nederland, Colo. 7.5′
   U.S.G.S. East Portal, Colo. 7.5′
   U.S.G.S. Fraser, Colo. 7.5′

In 1865, after the Civil War, a group of itinerant Mormons struggled to cross the Front Range through Boulder Pass, painstakingly dismantling their thirty-nine wagons and packing them piece by piece up the final leg of the journey. They were led by John Quincy Adams Rollins, who began construction of the Boulder Pass Wagon Road the following year. Rollins finished the road in 1873 and established a supply route over the pass which now bears his name. Years later David H. Moffat directed his Denver, Northwestern & Pacific Railway Company to construct a line over the same pass. Intended as a temporary route until completion of the Moffat Tunnel, this tortuous hill route served as main line for nearly a quarter of a century.

The tour route passes the old Boulder Pass Wagon Road and follows the railroad line, now the Moffat Road, on an adventurous climb over Rollins Pass. An alternate starting point from Lake Eldora Ski Area allows access to a scenic trail over Bryan and Guinn Mountains and saves about two hours time and a great deal of energy. Storms in the high alpine life zone near Rollins Pass can be dangerously severe and a clear day is mandatory for the crossing. *Do not leave the protection of trees if weather threatens!* The tour requires a drop-off car at either Peterson Lake or Lake Eldora Ski Area and a pick-up car at Winter Park Ski Area.

Drive on Colorado 119 southwest of Nederland; turn north onto the Eldora Road and after 1.5 miles fork left toward Lake Eldora Ski Area. Continue up Tennessee Mountain to either the east end of Peterson Lake or the ski area. Off-the-road parking is usually kept open near the east end of Peterson Lake.

From Peterson Lake ski to the Guinn Mountain Hut following the tour description for Guinn Mountain (No. 10), then proceed toward Rollins Pass beginning with paragraph seven of this tour.

From the Lake Eldora Ski Area buy a one-ride ticket and take the Canonball Chairlift (#1) to the top of the mountain. Make the easy climb northwest over The Pipeline ski run to Corona Massif, the top of the ski area. From the Gazebo warming hut here, a magnificent view extends west to towering Front Range mountains. Look for the long, steep-sided cirque that dips toward Forest Lakes west-southwest and pick out majestic James Peak on the skyline south-southwest. Pick up the old pipeline roadcut west of the warming hut and proceed toward the north-facing slope of Bryan

Panoramic view near Guinn Mountain

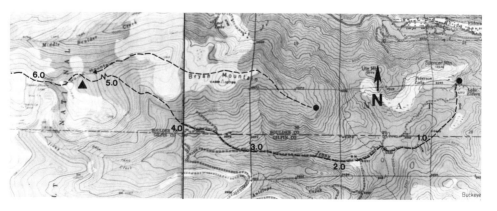

Mountain. The road soon narrows to a footpath and crosses a windy, sometimes snowbare, boulder field. This high lookout point gives a bird's-eye view of tour routes that begin from the town of Eldora and follow a network of winding valleys west (No.'s. 12-16).

Pass several pitch stumps, which still remain from a forest fire that swept this region near the turn of the century, destroying an estimated 70,000 acres of virgin forest. Intercept the wide pipeline cut again. Glide over wind-packed snow to the south side of Bryan Mountain and climb through scattered sub-alpine fir toward the east peak of Guinn Mountin. The deep Jenny Creek drainage and the range of snow-capped mountains south come into view from the southfacing mountainside. This view is soon cut off by stands of spruce and fir as the tour route follows the pipeline cut along the ridgetop west. Pass a crumbling, snow-drifted log cabin north of the cut and climb and drop through the snow fields to the Guinn Mountain Hut. Constructed by the Colorado Mountain Club and maintained cooperatively by its users, the cozy cabin provides an ideal overnight shelter for this tour, operating on the basis of club members first, visitors second.

From the hut break trail west through deep snow on the ridgetop. Curve south as the mountainside drops to a rocky ravine, and cross a wind-swept clearing on the southwest side of Guinn Mountain. Glide over the causeway high above Yankee Doodle Lake and make a careful climb west along the steep edge of the bowl to the Moffat Road, avoiding the even steeper slope farther north. Follow this easy-to-see roadcut as it climbs gradually north, then contour west and southwest along the steep south wall of the South Fork Middle Boulder Creek valley. Constant high winds often strip the roadbed clear of snow on this side of the pass but the drudgery of hiking is offset by a spectacular vista of the snowy Front Range mountains north. Soon pass a few standing timbers, several collapsed beams, and a wind-swept cinderbed that mark the site of the old Corona Station and Hotel. Built by Moffat's Denver, Northwestern & Pacific Railway Company, this station was named after the Spanish word for "crown" and seems indeed to sit on top of the world.

Glide south along the railroad bed over the frozen, wind-eroded waves of snow, pass high above the barely-discernible bowls of Pumphouse and Deadman Lakes, and ski by the half-buried posts of an old telegraph line. More than once a train would become stranded in a severe blizzard here and the railroad men would have to feel their way along the telegraph wires to shelter. Contour southwest over the vast, open range, then turn south and make a long downhill run to timberline. Pass the cross-posts of Corona Range Study Plot and break trail through deeper, softer snow on the sheltered roadcut to Riflesight Notch. The thick conifers throughout this area provide excellent shelter for an overnight camp.

Ski over Loop Trestle, then immediately turn south from the roadbed and make a steep drop to the South Fork Ranch Creek basin. Stay south of the creekbed and downhill through the trees to a large meadow. Pick up the Moffat Road at the west end of the meadow and contour gradually down the mountainside, staying high above the creek basin. As the road bends southwest the white-capped Front Range peaks near Berthoud Pass come into view above the distant Fraser River valley south. Follow the Moffat Road several miles to an intersection with the Aqueduct Road. Fork left, drop quickly through the Wolverine Creek drainage, then continue a more gradual descent south. The lower part of the Aqueduct Road is usually plowed but with only a few inches of snow it provides very fast skiing. Switchback west before coming to Buck Creek and drop quickly to the U.S. 40 highway near Winter Park Ski Area.

Wind-scoured Moffat road

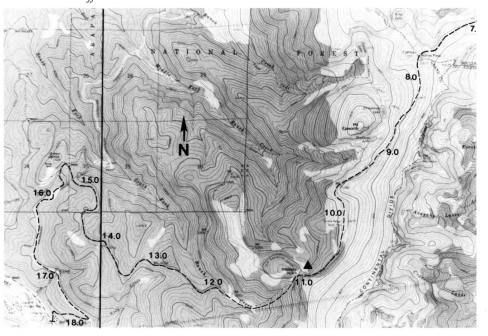

12 LOST LAKE

One day trip
Classification: Intermediate to Advanced
Distance: 3.0 miles one way
Skiing time: 2-2½ hours one way
Elevation gain: 960 feet
Maximum elevation: 9,800 feet
Season: Mid-December through March
Topographic map:
 U.S.G.S. Nederland, Colo. 7.5′

In 1893, the mountain settlement of Hesse, supported by rich silver mines near Lost Lake, contained a school, post office, sawmill, two stores and about a dozen cabins. However, the veins were gradually exhausted and the once-bustling mining camp changed to a ghost town. The ski touring trail passes by the few remaining Hesse buildings and then retraces the old mining road to Lost Lake.

Lost Lake lies couched on the bare north side of Bryan Mountain. An old mine shaft protrudes from the mountainside west and yellow tailings color the snow southeast. After a new snow, Lost Lake holds true to its name; thick conifers, more than are indicated on the 1942 Nederland topo, conceal the last turn south, necessitating a careful search for the old roadbed.

On Colorado 119 drive to the Eldora turnoff southwest of Nederland. Turn north and proceed through the Middle Boulder Creek valley, keeping right at 1.5 miles as the Lake Eldora Ski Area road forks left. Continue just through the town of Eldora to the end of the plowed road; turn around and park single file on the south side of the road.

Ski west on the wide, snow-covered road which runs along the north side of Middle Boulder Creek. Sidestep up the small drifted hill near the start, then glide over the almost-level valley floor. At 0.8 mile the Fourth of July Road (No. 16) branches right; keep left past a cabin and outbuildings, drop slightly, and continue to the Hesse townsite. Pass several old cabins on the right, ski into the aspen and douglas fir, then cross a bridge over North Fork Creek.

Cross a cleared area for a car turn-around and continue to an open hillside with a private cabin at the far end. Stay at the east end, turn slightly right toward the Chittenden Mountain peak, and climb through the aspen. Spiral west up the steep hillside immediately below the few evergreens on the north side, then climb steadily southwest on the road to the west side of the clearing.

Wind through the trees over level terrain, then drop into the South Fork drainage and cross the creek on a narrow footbridge. Follow the creek south and west, weave through the thick willows in the Lost Lake Creek drainage, and climb over the drifted hilltop. A few yards farther a sign marks the turn to Lost Lake Mining Camp; the jeep road bends sharply around granite boulders and continues on an east-facing hillside to a large shrubby meadow. Ski west about 150 yards along the south side of the meadow and find an inconspicuous jeep road south through the trees. Climb on the road, curving east to Lost Lake.

For the return trip drop slowly down the South Fork ravine, avoiding the windscoured roadbed south of the footbridge, then retrace the ski tracks.

Lost Lake

34

Looking west from Lost Lake turnoff

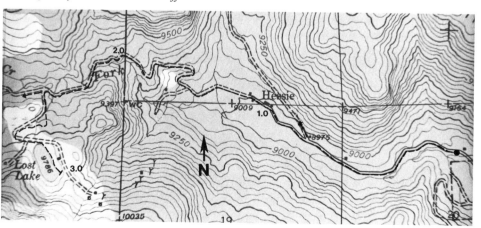

13 KING LAKE TRAIL

One day trip
Classification: Intermediate to Advanced
Distance: 5.9 miles one way
Skiing time: 3½-4½ hours one way
Elevation gain: 2,040 feet
Maximum elevation: 10,880 feet
Season: Mid December through April
Topographic maps:
  U.S.G.S. Nederland, Colo. 7.5′
  U.S.G.S. East Portal, Colo. 7.5′

Steep sides of the mountain range west form a box canyon around a snow-covered marsh, marking a definite end to the King Lake trail. King Lake, 450 feet higher west, remains unseen but the tour itself along the South Fork of Middle Boulder Creek provides its own reward: an easy climb up through tall englemann spruce and a smooth return trip down the creekbed. Except for the spiral climb at 1.4 miles the trail is never steep, making a good intermediate tour when the snow is fast.

Drive on Colorado 119 to the Eldora turnoff southwest of Nederland. Turn north and proceed through the Middle Boulder Creek valley, keeping right at 1.5 miles as the Lake Eldora Ski Area road forks left. Continue just through the town of Eldora to the end of the plowed road; turn around and park single file on the south side of the road.

Ski west on the wide, snow-covered road, keeping left at 0.8 mile as the Fourth of July Road (No. 16) branches right. Continue through the Hesse Townsite clearing, cross the bridge over North Fork Creek, and pass through a car turn-around clearing. Turn slightly right at the east end of an open hillside and climb through the aspen. Spiral west up the steep hillside then continue the steady climb southwest.

Wind west on the road through the trees, then cross the South Fork Creek on a narrow, snow-filled footbridge. Stay left of the creek, following it south then west. Cross through the willows in the Lost Lake Creek drainage and climb west over the drifted crest of the hill, soon passing the south turn to Lost Lake (No. 12). Glide west 0.2 mile farther over level terrain to another fork marking the King Lake trailhead. The clearing on the north usually holds snow when the road has been windswept.

Angle left, staying north of South Fork Creek, and ski into the blue spruce and lodgepole pine forest. Break into a clearing, marked by old stumps. From this point Guinn Mountain's broad sparsely-timbered north side can be seen. Cross the clearing and continue cross-country either skiing through the less timbered area about 200 yards north of the creekbed or skiing up the creekbed itself. Continue the gradual but steady climb, passing the unique circular bare spot on Guinn Mountain.

As the trees open to the immediate south, ski down to the creekbed and continue west on either side. The view north, earlier blocked by trees, now shows the forested top and thinly-timbered south side of Woodland Mountain. Glide through the tall spruce and pine and after 4.5 miles enter an increasingly narrower canyon. Stay off the two steep avalanche paths to the south that cut through the trees to the creek. Above the avalanche paths the log debris of the historic Moffat Road can be seen extending down the barren range. Continue up the drainage to a flat marsh area where a steep mountainside west ends the tour. Return down the creekbed.

Trail to King Lake

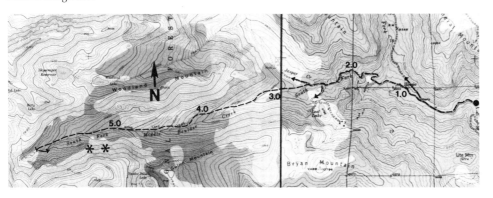

14 WOODLAND LAKE

One day trip
Classification: Advanced
Distance: 5.3 miles one way
Skiing time: 4-4½ hours one way
Elevation gain: 2,140 feet
Maximum elevation: 10,980 feet
Season: Mid-December through April
Topographic maps:
    U.S.G.S. Nederland, Colo. 7.5'
    U.S.G.S. East Portal, Colo. 7.5'

A ski tourer can carve christies for 200 yards on the smooth, wind-hardened snow of Woodland Lake's lee side, then ride the sudden bumps and fast drops down the creekbed. An advanced cross-country climb through englemann spruce to the timberline lake provides warm-up for the exhilerating downhill run. Find a lunch spot in the sheltering trees before climbing above timberline to Woodland Lake.

Drive on Colorado 119 to the Eldora turnoff southwest of Nederland. Turn north and proceed through the Middle Boulder Creek valley, keeping right at 1.5 miles as the Lake Eldora Ski Area road forks left. Continue just through the town of Eldora to the end of the plowed road; turn around and park single file on the south side of the road.

Ski west on the wide, snow-covered road, keeping left at 0.8 mile as the Fourth of July Road (No. 16) branches right. Continue through the Hesse Townsite clearing, cross the bridge over North Fork creek, and pass through a car turn-around clearing. Turn slightly right at the east end of an open hillside and climb through the aspens. Spiral west up the hillside continuing the steady climb southwest. Wind west on the road through the trees, then cross the South Fork creek on a narrow, snow-filled footbridge. Stay left of the creek, following it south then west. Cross through the willows in the Lost Lake creek drainage and climb west over the drifted crest of the hill, soon passing the south turn to Lost Lake (No. 12).

Glide west over level terrain keeping right where a sign soon marks the left fork to the King Lake Trail (No. 13). If wind has stripped the clearing of snow, follow the more protected tree-line along the south end. Ski through a short section of lodgepole pine and englemann spruce; pass two mine pits with mounds of yellow-orange tailings. Near the mines, bottom logs of an old cabin are visible when snow is thin. Ski cross-country northwest through scattered pines, staying close to the northeast side of Woodland Mountain. The roadbed ends near an inconspicuous junction of Woodland Lake Creek and Jasper Creek; a sign indicates the Woodland Lake Cutoff and Devils Thumb Trailhead (No. 15).

Intercept Woodland Lake creekbed; turn west and climb the wide ravine floor to a steep mountainside, passing two roofless log cabin ruins. Traverse the mountainside, staying away from avalanche danger on the steepest side. Climb cross-country on the north side of the creekbed through englemann spruce; then break out of the trees to an open windswept area and ski the final 0.3 mile through stunted conifers to Woodland Lake. Return down the creekbed avoiding the wind holes in the snow.

38

Woodland Lake

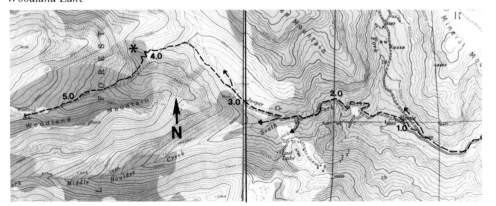

15 DEVILS THUMB LAKE

One day trip
Classification: Advanced
Distance: 6.8 miles one way
Skiing time: 4½-5 hours one way
Elevation gain: 2,320 feet
Maximum elevation: 11,160 feet
Season: Mid-December through April
Topographic maps:
   U.S.G.S. Nederland, Colo. 7.5'
   U.S.G.S. East Portal, Colo. 7.5'

Viewed from Jasper Creek, Devils Thumb towers high and alone on a silent sentinel over Devils Thumb Pass; seen from Devils Thumb Lake, however, the pointed spire combines with two other triangular flatirons to form a massive three-fingered devils paw. The tour's greater distance and elevation gain require an early starting time; the downhill return trip, however, takes about half the time as the uphill climb. Wind protection is needed for the final 0.5 mile above timberline.

Drive on Colorado 119 to the Eldora turnoff southwest of Nederland. Turn north and proceed through the Middle Boulder Creek valley, keeping right at 1.5 miles as the Lake Eldora Ski Area road forks left. Continue just through the town of Eldora to the end of the plowed road; turn around and park single file on the south side of the road.

Ski west on the wide, snow-covered road, keeping left at 0.8 mile as the Fourth of July Road (No. 16) branches right. Continue through the Hesse Townsite clearing; cross the bridge over North Fork creek; and pass through a car turn-around clearing. Turn slightly right at the east end of an open hillside and climb through the aspen. Spiral west up the hillside then continue the steady climb southwest. Wind west on the road through the trees, then cross the South Fork Creek on a narrow, snow-filled footbridge. Stay left of the creek, following it south then west. Cross through the

willows in the Lost Lake Creek drainage and climb west over the drifted crest of the hill, soon passing the south turn to Lost Lake (No. 12). Glide west over level terrain keeping right where a sign soon marks the left fork to the King Lake Trail (No. 13).

Ski northwest through a short section of lodgepole pine and englemann spruce; pass two mine pits and continue northwest, eventually crossing Jasper Creek and the left fork to Woodland Lake (No. 14). Follow Jasper Creek drainage through willows and scattered conifers toward the steep west end of Chittenden Mountain. As the ravine narrows switchback the less steep hillside west and either ski up the creekbed or climb the ridge north of the creekbed through tall, fire-burned tree trunks. Ski cross-country west through a denser englemann spruce forest and break into a meadow, marking the inconspicuous junction of creeks. Jasper Reservoir lies north up a steep well-timbered mountain and a round-topped peak rises south above the timberline.

Bend west as Jasper Creek angles southwest but stay left of the steeper mountainside north. Make the rigorous ascent up the mountainside to a stunning timberline vista of the Continental Divide: a protruding ridge rises west to a 12,123 foot peak, then the horizon line north drops to the broad saddle of Devils Thumb Pass. Curve north and maintain elevation through the few snow-laden trees; contour east around a rise and drop slightly to Devils Thumb Lake. Return over the same route or follow the creekbed east from Devils Thumb Lake and pass south of Jasper Reservoir, staying high through the trees.

Orientation on the trail

40

Willows along the trail

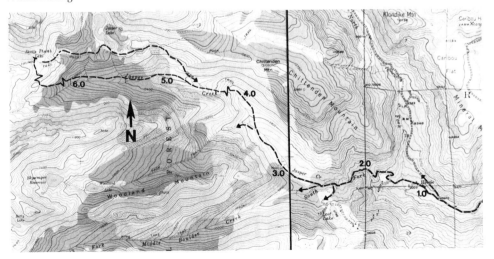

41

16 FOURTH OF JULY CAMPGROUND

One day trip
Classification: Beginner to Intermediate
Distance: 5.0 miles one way
Skiing time: 3½-4 hours one way
Elevation gain: 1,320 feet
Maximum elevation: 10,160 feet
Season: January through March
Topographic maps:
  U.S.G.S. Nederland, Colo. 7.5′
  U.S.G.S. East Portal, Colo. 7.5′

In 1875, mule trains wound their way up the valley between Chittenden and Bald Mountains with supplies for the Fourth of July Mine at the base of South Arapaho Peak. After a few years the silver vein was exhausted but in 1900 the mine was reopened to produce rich copper ore. Today deep snow in the valley still holds back the world of mechanized transport and the frosted signs at Buckingham Campground reading "No Parking This Side" are the only reminder that times have changed.

The wide, snow-covered roadbed to Fourth of July Campground climbs very gradually, making the tour perfect for beginners and families. If windy, stop for lunch before skiing the last mile in the unprotected valley. On a quiet, moonlit night the smooth road is quite easy to follow.

On Colorado 119 drive to the Eldora turnoff southwest of Nederland. Turn north and proceed through the Middle Boulder Creek valley, keeping right at 1.5 miles as the Lake Eldora Ski Area road forks left. Continue just through the town of Eldora to the end of the plowed road; turn around and park single file on the south side of the road.

Begin skiing west on the unplowed road, sidestep up a small, drifted hill near the start, and glide on the flat trail north of Middle Boulder Creek. Fork right at 0.8 mile onto the Fourth of July Road and pass a cabin and outbuildings. Soon the picturesque Hesse Townsite is visible, then becomes smaller and smaller as the road continues a steady climb southeast toward Chittenden Mountain. On Bryan Mountain, across the valley, miniature alpine skiers maneuver around moguls on the steep ski slope.

Swing north around Chittenden Mountain, pass several private cabins, and enter a small clearing near the 2.0 mile mark. Break trail through deep snow in the clearing, then veer northwest toward North Fork Creek. Ski through a section of willow and aspen which mark the branch creek from Chittenden Mountain. Angle northwest again, glide along the south side of Klondike Mountain, and wind west through more trees, crossing the creek drainage from Bald Mountain. The roadbed soon bends toward the North Fork Creek and enters an increasingly narrower canyon.

Ski through a long meadow, pass several more private cabins, and re-enter the conifers. The road continues to a treeless and often windy valley. Continue cross-country under the rugged and massive Bald Mountain range, pass the half-buried picnic tables of Buckingham Campground, and drop slightly west into the trees at Fourth of July Campground. With the wind at the tourer's back and a broken downhill trail, the smooth-gliding return trip takes one-half the time as the trip in.

Fourth of July campground

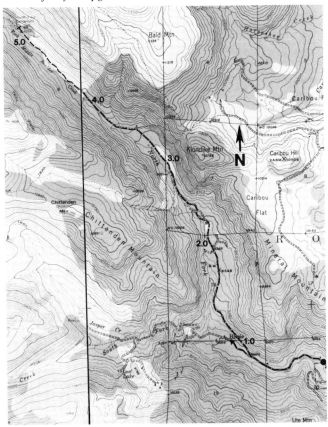

17 LEFTHAND PARK RESERVOIR

Half-day trip
Classification: Beginner
Distance: 2.1 miles one way
Skiing time: 1-1½ hours one way
Elevation gain: 600 feet
Maximum elevation: 10,680 feet
Season: Mid-December through April
Topographic map:
   U.S.G.S. Ward, Colo. 7.5'

Massive Niwot Ridge sprawls more than five miles eastward from the Indian Peaks Range, shadowing Lefthand Park Reservoir 900 feet below its east end. Niwot means left-handed in Arapaho; it was the name of a Southern Arapaho chieftain, an important leader of his people from 1889 to the early 1900's, who reportedly was left-handed because he had lost the fingertips of his right hand. Ironically however, Lefthand Creek which runs east from Lefthand Park Reservoir had been named for a fur trader, southpaw Andrew Sublette, long before Chief Niwot became known to white men.

The tour to Lefthand Park Reservoir follows the wide summer road for all but the last 0.1 mile. An additional climb up the north mountainside of Niwot Ridge rewards the tourer with a view of Little Pawnee Peak and Mount Audubon.

Drive on Colorado 72 north of Ward to the Brainard Lake turnoff; turn west and proceed 2.6 miles to the guard station at the end of the plowed road. This access road occasionally is closed by drifts so be prepared with tire chains, shovel and sand. A turn-around and parking space is plowed out for many cars.

Begin skiing from a sign reading "Lefthand Park Reservoir 2" on the south side of the parking area. Stay above Lefthand Creek and climb south over a snow drift into the trees. Follow the wide lodgepole-lined road, soon curving west and gradually climbing around two switchbacks. Scraggly limber pine cling to the exposed roadbank.

The road heads southwest, then swings south and bridges Lefthand Creek. Small englemann spruce seedlings poke through the snow around the creek basin. Resume a southwest direction and climb over the snow drifts in the road. Vibrant yellow-orange willows replace the englemann spruce as the road breaks into a more open area. As the road ends, glide cross-country west into the long, snow bowl of Lefthand Park Reservoir, passing a huge pile of bulldozed logs at the east end.

Cross to the southwest end of the Reservoir and climb the north Niwot mountainside to a lookout at treeline. Cloud shadows dip and roll from Little Pawnee Peak's long ridge to Mount Audubon's bald dome. Shuss to the Reservoir bottom and retrace the ski tracks to the parking area.

Trail scene

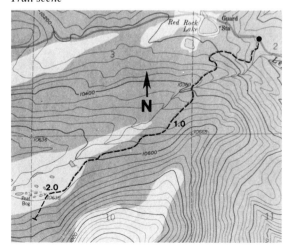

18 BRAINARD LAKE

Half-day trip
Classification: Beginner
Distance: 2.0 miles one way
Skiing time: 1-1½ hours one way
Elevation gain: 280 feet
Maximum elevation: 10,360 feet
Season: Mid-December through March
Topographic map:
  U.S.G.S. Ward, Colo. 7.5'

Late evening sun still glistens from the high bald dome and cirque of Mount Audubon long after the valleys darken, casting vivid shadows down the mountainside. Mount Audubon, Little Pawnee Peak, and mountains more distant in the Indian Peaks Range west can be seen at different times during much of the tour; a vast panorama, however, confronts the tourer east of Brainard Lake. Pyramid-shaped Kiowa Peak juts southwest above rocky, snow-laced Niwot Ridge and a jagged saddle loops from Arikaree Peak to Navajo Peak west-southwest. Farther west Shoshoni and Apache Peaks appear in a cluster of pointed spires; Little Pawnee Peak rises west and Mount Audubon dominates the view northwest.

Noisy gray jays or "camprobbers," common in the Brainard Lake area, often accompany the tourer throughout the day, giving raucous reminders from every other tree to stop and share lunch. On midwinter weekends the Colorado Mountain Club cabin northwest of Brainard Lake makes a popular lunch spot; the Club opens the cabin and serves hot drinks to the many ski tourers.

When windstorms have scoured the wide, unprotected Brainard Lake road, the narrow, tree-lined North and South CMC Trails (No. 19) offer better touring. Often weather conditions improve in late February and March with less wind and heavier snows; a clear day after

new snow makes for exceptional touring on the wide road.

Although the tour to Brainard Lake rises above 10,000 feet elevation, the steep climb comes during the drive to the starting point; the tour itself, except for a drift at the start, remains near-level all the way.

Drive on Colorado 72 north of Ward to the Brainard Lake turnoff; turn west and proceed 2.6 miles to the end of the plowed road. The access road occasionally is closed by drifts so carry tire chains, shovel, and sand. A turnaround and parking space is maintained for many cars.

Ski west on the wide road, immediately passing through two gates. Climb a large snow drift and break into a meadow area. After 0.2 mile detour south on a side road for an exploration of Red Rock Lake and vista of the Indian Peaks Range west. Limber pine grow in interesting shapes on the east side of the lake.

Glide west on the main road, skirting north of a spacious open area. East of Brainard Lake the road forks: the right fork passes a campground, then swings north around the lake, bridging ever-flowing South St. Vrain Creek; the left fork continues on the main road, not shown on the 1957 Ward topo, south around the lake.

Continue on either fork northwest of Brainard Lake, and cut back east on a flagged trail to the CMC cabin. Return over the ski tracks or on the North or South CMC Trail.

Indian Peaks Range from Red Rock Lake

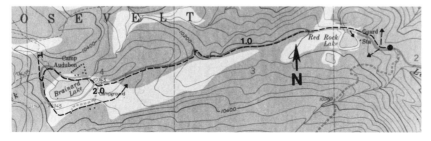

19 NORTH AND SOUTH CMC TRAILS

One day trip
Classification: Beginner
Distances:
  2.6 miles one way — North Trail
  2.7 miles one way — South Trail
Skiing time: 1½-2 hours one way
Elevation gain: 400 feet
Maximum elevation: 10,480 feet
Season: Mid-December through April
Topographic map:
  U.S.G.S. Ward, Colo. 7.5'

The Boulder Group of the Colorado Mountain Club (CMC) has cut and flagged two new ski touring trails through the trees, paralleling the summer road (No. 18) north and south to Brainard Lake and the CMC cabin. Spruce and fir trees block the view along much of the winding path but also protect the snow from winter winds. The North Trail contains short, exciting shusses and easy climbs while the South Trail remains very level and fast. Heavy trail use on midwinter weekends result in a confusion of criss-crossing tracks and require the orientation of the Ward topo map.

Drive on Colorado 72 north of Ward to the Brainard Lake turnoff; turn west and proceed 2.6 miles to the guard station at the end of the plowed road. This access road occasionally is closed by drifts so be prepared with tire chains, shovel and sand. A turn-around and parking space is plowed out for many cars.

Begin skiing west on the Brainard Lake summer road, passing a gate and a flagged left fork to the South Trail. Turn right about twenty feet east of a second post-and-cable gate onto the North Trail. Follow the red flags north and

northeast through the spruce and fir; then swing west. Soon the trees north open slightly to a view of the broad, forested South St. Vrain valley: a long, round mountain, then two matching peaks rise above the far side, and the distant plains down the valley east shimmer on the hazy horizon. Continue west across the creek from Red Rock Lake and through the north end of a clearing. Bright green moss, popularly called Old Man's Beard, hang in interesting shapes from much of the spruce and fir, a characteristic of shady, north-facing slopes.

climbing and dropping through the many drainages. Then it swings northwest and crosses the wide, snow-filled South St. Vrain Creek. Ski across the clearing just beyond the creek and climb through the wide-spaced trees to the South St. Vrain Trail. Turn left, cross a branch creek, and continue west on the flagged trail. Curve gradually south following the blazed trees, cross the east end of a meadow, and ski west to the CMC cabin.

For the return route on the South Trail intercept the summer road west of the CMC cabin and ski south on the road around the west end of Brainard Lake. Leave the road at the clearing south of Brainard Lake and follow the red flags into the trees, passing an old camp site and the ruins of a stone fireplace. The trail heads east through a section of dead standing timber and englemann spruce.

Traverse a hillside, then ski cross-country as the trees open from meadow to meadow guided by the flags and limbed trees. Pass south of the smaller Red Rock Lake through wind-twisted limber pine and double pole the long, gentle drop to the parking area.

48

Near the trailhead

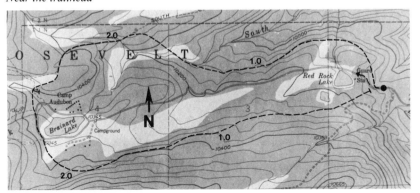

20 LONG LAKE AND LAKE ISABELLE

One day trip
Classification: Intermediate
Distance: 4.6 miles one way
Skiing time: 3-3½ hours one way
Elevation gain: 800 feet
Season: Mid-December through April
Topographic map:
  U.S.G.S. Ward, Colo. 7.5'

On a snowy day the white, treeless banks of Lake Isabelle's elongated bowl limit depth perception to a few feet and a downhill plunge from the east lip to the lake bottom produces an eerie feeling of suspended motion. On a clear day, however, glistening white mountains in the Indian Peaks Range tower west above the smooth bowl.

The snow depth in the South St. Vrain creekbed — deep enough to retrieve last summer's fishhooks and lures from the tree branches — makes a clear, flat avenue to Long Lake. Above Long Lake the cross-country trail through tree clusters rises almost as slowly but the final 0.2 mile to Lake Isabelle climbs sharply around a steep knoll.

Drive on Colorado 72 north of Ward to the Brainard Lake turnoff; turn west and proceed 2.6 miles to the guard station at the end of the plowed road. A turn-around and parking space is cleared for many cars.

Ski to the west end of Brainard Lake on the North CMC Trail (No. 19), the Brainard Lake Trail (No. 18), or the South CMC Trail. For the South CMC Trail begin skiing west from the parking area on the Brainard Lake road; pass the first roadgate and turn left into the trees before the second gate at the flagged trailhead. Follow the straight, flagged trail up a gentle hill, then bend southwest, passing south of the smaller Red Rock Lake. Continue cross-country, using the flags and limbed trees as a guide. The trail eventually traverses a hillside and passes through a section of dead standing timber.

Ski through an old campsite with stone fireplace ruins; glide north across a clearing south of Brainard Lake to the road. Follow the road around the west end of Brainard Lake, passing the half-buried picnic tables of the Niwot picnic area. A few hundred yards past the picnic area turn west up South St. Vrain Creek, the first break in the trees. Wind west on the wide creekbed through big douglas fir and englemann spruce; maintain elevation as trees south eventually give way to a rolling meadow and continue to the east end of Long Lake. From this open vantage point the eastern-most end of Little Pawnee Peak comes into view northwest and the snow streaked face of Niwot Ridge looms skyward south.

Glide across the lengthy expanse of Long Lake; bend west and ski cross-country around the tree clusters, staying low in the South St. Vrain drainage. After one-half mile from Long Lake break clear from the trees to a view west of Lake Isabelle's protruding east lip. A rocky knoll with avalanche runs on either side rises from the South St. Vrain valley. Continue west and gradually climb above the low brushy area under the rocky knoll. Turn northwest around the knoll and switchback through the wide-spaced trees, avoiding the avalanche paths. Cut south at the top of the knoll to the east lip of Lake Isabelle. The bowl drops below, and the steep, white sides rise to the range from Shoshoni Peak north and to Niwot Ridge south.

Double pole to the lake bottom and continue west for a better view of the Indian Peaks Range. Return over the same route, shussing the hillside north of the avalanche area.

Snow-covered sign on Long Lake Trail

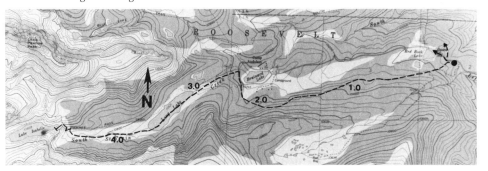

21 MITCHELL AND BLUE LAKES

One day trip
Classification: Advanced
Distance: 5.1 miles one way
Skiing time: 3½-4 hours one way
Elevation gain: 1,240 feet
Maximum elevation: 11,320 feet
Season: Mid-December through April
Topographic map:
  U.S.G.S. Ward, Colo. 7.5'

The tour to Blue Lake, the most challenging in the Brainard Lake area, follows the valley between Mount Audubon and Little Pawnee Peak to a giant amphitheater formed by Paiute Peak, Mount Toll, and Pawnee Peak. On the return trip a seemingly endless downhill drop through open snow meadows is reward for the arduous climb. The Blue Lake summer trail disappears in winter but the creekbed from Blue Lake provides a clear path. Carry adequate wind protection for the tour and pick a lunch spot before climbing above the sheltering trees around Mitchell Lake.

Drive on Colorado 72 north of Ward to the Brainard Lake turnoff; turn west and proceed 2.6 miles to the guard station at the end of the plowed road. This access road occasionally is closed by drifts so be prepared with tire chains, shovel and sand. A turn-around and parking space is plowed out for many cars.

Ski to the summer road west of the Colorado Mountain Club cabin either on the South CMC Trail (No. 19), the Brainard Lake Trail (No. 18), or the North CMC Trail. For the North CMC Trail begin skiing west on the Brainard Lake summer road; turn right about twenty feet east of the second post-and-cable gate and follow the red flags through spruce and fir trees. Continue west across the creek from Red Rock Lake and through the north end of a clearing.

Turn west-southwest and climb and drop through the rolling terrain, then swing northwest and cross South St. Vrain Creek. Ski across a clearing and climb to the open cut of the South St. Vrain Trail. Turn left, cross a branch creek and continue west on the flagged trail. Curve gradually south, then break into the east end of a wind-swept meadow. Ski west through the meadow eventually crossing the road to Mitchell Lake trailhead parking.

Continue west across the shrubby, wind-packed meadow to the Mitchell Lake creekbed at the northwest end. Climb cross-country up the drainage; turn west out of the trees and ski along the south side of an open area to Mitchell Lake. Cross to the south tributary and climb up the wide ravine to an open, flat mesa. Here twisted, low lying sub-alpine fir struggle against the high wind.

Turn northwest, staying well north of Little Pawnee Peak's rocky hillside, and contour east around a protruding ridgetop to Blue Lake Creek. Follow the creekbed to timberline Blue Lake. For the return trip, ski north of the creekbed route maintaining elevation on the Mount Audubon mountainside. Then telemark and double pole east down the long, open snow meadows to Mitchell Lake and follow the tracks out.

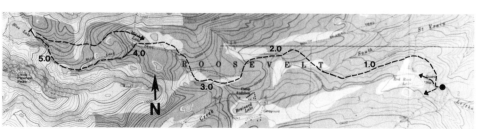

22 FINCH LAKE AND PEAR RESERVOIR

One day trip
Classification: Advanced
Distance: 6.3 miles one way
Skiing time: 4-4½ hours one way
Elevation gain: 1,840 feet
Maximum elevation: 10,600 feet
Season: Mid-December through mid-April
Topographic map:
  U.S.G.S. Allens Park, Colo. 7.5′

A trip to Finch Lake and Pear Reservoir requires proper ski wax, orienteering skill, and good endurance. Proper wax makes easier the arduous climb up Meadow Mountain. Keen use of a map and compass simplifies the confusing drainage area near the 3.0 mile mark. And good endurance is necessary for the last series of switchbacks below Pear Reservoir. Beautiful vistas of Mount Meeker, Pagoda Mountain, and Chiefs Head Peak more than compensate for the challenging trail. The trees around the flat Finch Lake meadow are an ideal stopping place for lunch.

Drive on Colorado 7 to the Allens Park turnoff; turn south and continue another 0.1 mile to an intersection marked by the Com-munity Church of Allenspark. Proceed west and park off the road below the "Y". Hike one block south on Gordon Street, turn west again, and continue on the winding jeep road, staying north of Willow Creek.

Begin skiing on the snow-filled roadbed immediately past the last house. Swing west and ski by the bulletin board at the Park boundary. The trail immediately narrows to a six foot wide path and crosses indiscernable Fox Creek. Herringbone and sidestep up the steep hillside, then drop into a dense fir forest. Cross a small drainage, ski back into the lodgepole pine, and continue west on the rising and falling path. Climb through a burned area now covered with aspen and spruce. Through the trees snow-capped Mount Meeker, Pagoda Mountain, and Chiefs Head Peak form the northern wall of sprawling Wild Basin.

Double pole a short drop to the Wild Basin Trail junction, turn south, and climb steadily up Meadow Mountain. As the trail becomes increasingly indistinct near a branch of North St. Vrain Creek, depend on a map and compass and follow trees blazes and trimmed branches that mark the path. Ski over the footbridge that crosses a second branch of North St. Vrain Creek and cross-country west until the mountainside begins to fall steeply northwest. Timber-bash through the dense trees to flat, snow-covered Finch Lake.

Glide to the southwest end of Finch Lake and continue through the open meadow area. Turn west to Cony Creek as the trees close in, then ski up the creekbed. Leave the creekbed at a long, brush-filled meadow area and cross-country west. Re-enter the trees, and soon come to a branch creek. Follow to the right of the branch creek; switchback a steep hillside and ski west through wind-stunted trees on the open, lee side of Finch Reservoir. Mount Copeland northwest and Elk Tooth Mountain southwest form the large basin that empties into Finch Reservoir. Return over the ski tracks.

Stone dam at Pear Reservoir

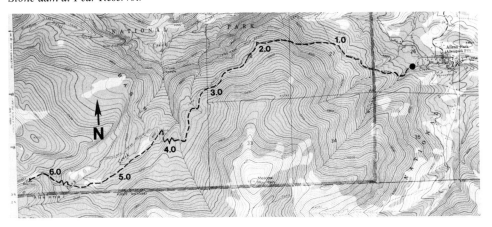

23 CALYPSO CASCADES AND OUZEL FALLS

One day trip
Classification: Beginner to Intermediate
Distance: 4.7 miles one way
Skiing time: 2½-3 hours one way
Elevation gain: 1,080 feet
Maximum elevation: 9,400 feet
Season: January through March
Topographic map:
   U.S.G.S. Allens Park, Colo. 7.5'

Rocky Mountain National Park authorities recognize the flat Wild Basin floor as an excellent touring area and extend special courtesy to ski tourers with a sign at the Park entrance that requests non-skiers to stay out of the ski tracks. Although beginning skiers may prefer to stay on the road between Copeland Lake and the Wild Basin Ranger Station, tourers who can manage an intermediate downhill run are urged to continue beyond the Ranger Station to Calypso Cascades and Ouzel Falls. Excellent snow conditions exist on this shaded Thunder Lake Trail through March. On the basin floor, however, strong winds and generally warmer temperatures reduce the season to January and February.

Drive on Colorado 7 to the Wild Basin access road north of Allens Park, marked by a Wild Basin Ranger Station sign. Turn west onto the dirt road and proceed 0.5 mile to a parking area at the east end of Copeland Lake.

Begin skiing on the road around the south side of Copeland Lake; continue west through scattered ponderosa pine and soon pass the Rocky Mountain National Park boundary. Gradually curve southwest on the level road and ski past a meadow of beaver-cut aspen stumps. Stay left where two branch roads fork right to private property, then swing south and ski over the bridge across North St. Vrain Creek. Glide in and out of ponderosa pine and fir on the level Wild Basin floor, staying south of the creekbed. Cross another bridge and come to the Wild Basin Ranger Station parking area. The Ranger Station log cabin, usually locked during the winter, sits back in the trees at the north end.

Cross the bridge over Hunters Creek and pass a bulletin board with weather information, Park regulations, and a topographic map. Glide southwest on the road-sized Thunder Lake Trail, begin a gradual climb, and soon cross the bridge over Sandbeach Creek. Continue on a shaded trail and after crossing the North St. Vrain Creek ski more directly south to the Cony Creek crossing. The quiet, snow-laden boulders of Calypso Cascades above the Cony Creek bridge hold the promise for a noisy, splashing waterfall at spring thaw.

Follow the Thunder Lake Trail across another footbridge and stay close to the steep mountainside south on a gradual climb. Ski two steep hairpin turns, cross Ouzel Creek under the winter-stilled Ouzel Falls, and climb around a jutting ridge to a good vista and lunch spot. The expansive Wild Basin stretches back east-northeast; Meeker Ridge, streaked with glaciers, extends from Mt. Meeker north and a white dome caps forested Meadow Mountain southeast. The tour may be continued another 3.2 miles to Thunder Lake (No. 24).

Water stop

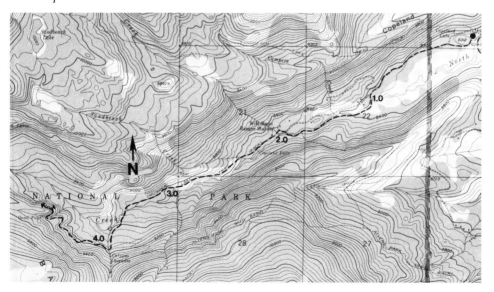

24 THUNDER LAKE

One day trip or overnight
Classification: Advanced
Distance: 7.9 miles one way
Skiing time: 4-5 hours one way
Elevation gain: 2,260 feet
Maximum elevation: 10,580 feet
Season: January through March
Topographic maps:
  U.S.G.S. Allens Park, Colo. 7.5′
  U.S.G.S. Isolation Peak, Colo. 7.5′

The last few miles of trail to Thunder Lake climbs the north Wild Basin wall for an excellent view southwest of round Mahana Peak and steep, rugged Tanima Peak. "Mahana" is the Taos Indians' word for the Comanche Indians, while "Tanima" represents one of the thirteen Comanche tribes. Although Comanches lived mostly south of the Arkansas River, the Indian place names for this area are particularly appropriate. Along with several other places in Wild Basin, the shores of Thunder Lake were an old Indian campsite.

With fast snow and good wax an "out and return" trip to Thunder Lake can be done in one long day but an overnight tour allows a more reasonable pace. Harsh weather discourages camping on the high bench around Thunder Lake but sheltered sites can be found one-half mile down North St. Vrain Creek.

Drive on Colorado 7 to the Wild Basin access road north of Allens Park, marked by a Wild Basin Ranger Station sign. Turn west onto the dirt road and proceed 0.5 mile to a parking area at the east end of Copeland Lake.

Ski around the south side of Copeland Lake, then follow the road west through the Rocky Mountain National Park boundary. Glide across the flat Wild Basin floor, staying left where branch roads fork right to private property. Cross the North St. Vrain Creek and continue through the pine and fir to the Wild Basin Ranger Station parking area. Ski over the bridge across Hunters Creek and pass a bulletin board with weather information, Park regulations, and a topographic map. The snowy trail begins a gradual climb, crosses Sandbeach Creek, and continues southwest through a forest.

After recrossing the North St. Vrain Creek, curve south and climb gradually toward the Calypso Cascade mountainside. Ski over two branches of Cony Creek, climb through a series of hairpin turns, and pass under quiet Ouzel Falls. Climb northeast around a jutting ridge to a good viewpoint of the expansive Wild Basin valley. Mount Meeker and glacier-streaked Meeker Ridge north highlight the panorama. Turn northwest from the view point and follow the trail under a protruding granite slab. Switchback closer to the basin bottom then traverse the steep mountainside. Pass a south fork to Bluebird Lake and glide over a rising and falling trail to the basin floor. After crossing the North St. Vrain Creek again begin a steep climb up the south side of Mount Orton. Soon scattered limber pine become mixed with the lodgepole pine as the trail enters the high sub-alpine life zone.

Pass a steep, northerly trail to Lion Lake and as the summer trailcut becomes hard to find, contour west on a cross-country route. Follow the curve of the mountainside northwest and continue a steep cross-country climb. Cross through the open meadows around two tributary creeks, glide west to the open lee side of Thunder Lake, and ski over wind-scoured snow to the lake bowl. Return over the ski tracks or down the North St. Vrain creekbed.

Mount Meeker

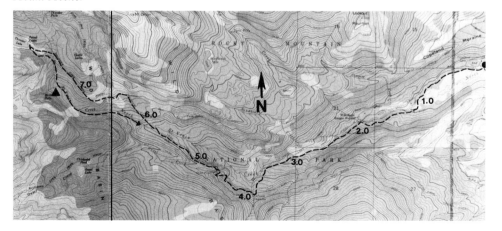

25 SANDBEACH LAKE

One day trip
Classification: Intermediate to Advanced
Distance: 4.2 miles one way
Skiing time: 3½-4 hours one way
Elevation gain: 2,000 feet
Maximum elevation: 10,320 feet
Season: January through March
Topographic map:
  U.S.G.S. Allens Park, Colo. 7.5'

The tour to Sandbeach Lake begins with a discouraging climb up the steep, often snow-bare, Copeland Moraine mountainside but once in the trees the trail conditions improve considerably. An inspiring vista of towering, rugged Mount Meeker and Pagoda Mountain makes the steep climb to the lake well worthwhile. With an elevation drop of 2,000 feet the return trip takes only half the time as the trip in.

Drive on Colorado 7 to the Wild Basin access road north of Allens Park, marked by a Wild Basin Ranger Station sign. Turn west onto the dirt road and proceed 0.5 mile to a parking area at the east end of Copeland Lake.

Cross the road north of Copeland Lake, climb a series of steep, wind-scoured switchbacks up Copeland Moraine, then follow the trail west on a steady climb. Pass a bulletin board with a topographic map and several signs of regulations at the Rocky Mountain National Park boundary and continue over a rising and falling trail to the Copeland Moraine ridgetop. Double pole down a slight drop onto the north-facing side of Copeland Moraine and ski west where a branch trail, marked by a sign with mileages, turns northeast to Meeker Park.

Traverse the side of Lookout Mountain, following blazed trees as the trail becomes confusing, then glide along the north side of Campers Creek through a stand of pine. After a steady climb up the mountainside, double pole west toward the creekbed and look for a small, snowy footbridge a few hundred feet from the beginning of the drop. Cross the creek near the footbridge, climb east on the trail, and soon switchback west. The conspicuous trail, lined by lodgepole and limber pine, continues west, cutting across the steep mountainside north of Hunters Creek.

Glide northwest to Hunters Creek where the trail becomes lost in an aspen grove. With the aid of a compass, sight a landmark due west on the mountainside and begin climbing on a cross-country course. Switchback through the scattered limber pine, staying well south of the Hunters Creek drainage; hold a westerly course as the terrain levels and intercept the wide, windblown Sandbeach Lake. A beautiful panorama of bald mountain peaks juts into the skyline northeast. Mount Orton, closest to the lake, forms one end of a vast amphitheater which extends north to Pagoda Mountain. Mount Meeker, bald and rounded, cuts an arc in the horizon line north. A return trip down the snow-crusted mountainside to Hunters Creek can be managed with sweeping telemark turns. Proceed over the ski tracks from the creekbed.

Pagoda Mountain

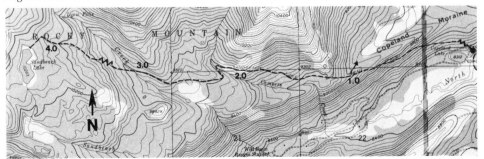

26 LONGS PEAK TRAIL

One day trip
Classification: Advanced
Distance: 2.0 miles one way
Skiing time: 2-2½ hours one way
Elevation gain: 1,260 feet
Maximum elevation: 10,660
Season: Mid-December through April
Topographic map:
  U.S.G.S. Longs Peak, Colo. 7.5'

The Longs Peak Trail switchbacks steeply from one shaded, level plateau to another, and finally breaks above wind-stunted englemann spruce to a lofty vista point of Longs Peak west and the Twin Sisters Peaks east. With proper mountaineering equipment and good weather the trip can be continued west to the flat meadowland around the Shelter House. This long extension presents a closer look at the rugged granite features of Longs Peak. However, dangerous weather conditions prevent the trip on most winter days. The Shelter House is LOCKED throughout the winter.

Drive on Colorado 7 to the Longs Peak Campground turnoff between Estes Park and Allenspark. Turn west onto the dirt road which is usually kept open by the Larimer County highway department and proceed 1.1 miles to the Longs Peak Trail parking area, turning left where the road branches right to the Longs Peak Campground.

Immediately west of the parking area a bulletin board with winter weather information, Park regulations, and a topographic map marks the trailhead. Begin skiing south on a gradual climb through lodgepole pine; switchback northwest and climb steeply up the winding path. Soon the trail levels and trees break away enough to allow a glimpse of the forested, granite-topped Estes Cone north-northwest. Resume the steep climb northwest through thick trees, then glide through a level aspen grove near the 0.5 mile mark and pass a north fork to Eugenia Mine.

Englemann spruce and fir mix with the lodgepole pine as the trail switchbacks south. Climb steadily up the Pine Ridge mountainside, swing close to Alpine Brook, then continue the steep traverse northwest. Cross the steep cut of an underground telephone line and proceed through another switchback. After the trail levels to the west, a view of rounded Mount Lady Washington and notched Longs Peak on the horizon southwest fills the openings between the trees. Pass an inconspicuous left fork to Goblins Forest Campsites and follow the straight path through a section of dead, grotesquely-shaped limber pine. The snow-filled trail climbs gradually, levels off and continues past a small meadow then under a boulder field.

Ski west next to Alpine Brook, dip southwest across tributary Larkspur Creek, and swing closer toward the Alpine Brook basin. Proceed up the steep, east-facing mountainside through six, short switchbacks and continue past giant spruce trees near the Alpine Brook crossing. Glide southwest through the crusty snow to a windy sub-alpine meadow of stunted conifers —a good stopping place. Here a splendid vantage point shows the Twin Sisters Peaks east across the deep Tahosa Valley. Sparkling buildings and straight roads pattern the flat plains farther east. Southwest the famous East Face of Longs Peak towers above the Chasm Lake bowl.

For a trip closer to Longs Peak, cache skis near Alpine Brook and follow the wind-swept trail south then west. After a hard climb up the boulder-strewn mountainside, turn south again where a branch trail forks north to Jims Grove. Continue along the precipitous north side of Mills Moraine, pass high above the deep pocket that contains Peacock Pool, and drop gradually to the locked Shelter House. Chasm Lake remains hidden in a higher cirque west but the massive granite wedge of the Ships Prow, the wide Notch, and the sheer East Face shape an awesome panorama. Return over the ski tracks.

Along the trail

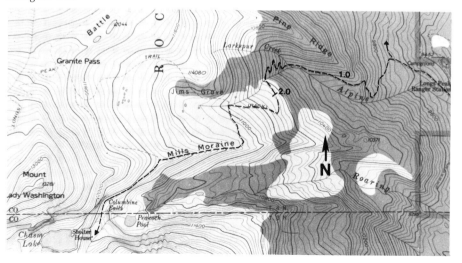

27 MOORE PARK

Half-day trip
Classification: Beginner to Intermediate
Distance: 1.7 miles one way
Skiing time: 1-1½ hours one way
Elevation gain: 455 feet
Maximum elevation: 9,860 feet
Season: January through March
Topographic map:
 U.S.G.S. Longs Peak, Colo. 7.5'

After an initial climb up Pine Ridge, the trail to open, peaceful Moore Park settles into an easy series of ups and downs. With good wax this short tour takes little more than an hour; it may be extended to a full day, however, by skiing down the north side of Battle Mountain via Storm Pass, intersecting the Glacier Creek Trail (No. 31), and continuing to Glacier Basin Campground. This extension adds 6.5 miles to the tour and requires a second car at Glacier Basin Campground turnoff.

The short distance to Moore Park allows time to stop at the Eugenia Mine site, poke around the mine ruins, and mentally reconstruct the scene when the mine was active during the early 1900's. Sawed timbers in Inn Brook once supported a track that penetrated 1,000 feet into the mountainside. A log cabin near the mine, now weathered and roofless, was the home of miner Carl P. Norwall and his two daughters. But not the usual spartan mining life for Mr. Norwall! Evenings were spent in the snug cabin with the musical refinement of a piano. This luxury together with his two daughters always seemed to attract a chorus of young men from neighboring lodges for the evening's gala.

Drive on Colorado 7 to the Longs Peak Campground access road, marked by a large Rocky Mountain National Park sign. Turn west onto the dirt road which is usually kept open by the Larimer County highway department, and proceed 1.1 miles to a large parking area, turning left where the road branches to the campground.

A bulletin board with winter information, park regulations, and a topographic map marks the trailhead. Begin skiing south on a gradual climb through lodgepole pine, then switchback northwest and climb steeply on the winding path. Soon the trail levels and trees separate enough to allow a view north of forested, granite-topped Estes Cone. Isolated from other mountains, this conspicuous cone was sculptured by erosion, evidence of the odd quirks of geomorphology.

Resume the steep climb northwest through thick trees, glide through a level aspen grove, and fork right to Eugenia Mine. Begin a gradual climb north up the Pine Ridge hillside. Soon the trail crests, winds downhill through a shallow gully, then climbs gradually again up the hillside. Curve northwest, drop slightly, and glide through a mixed conifer forest. Cross Inn Brook and detour west several yards up the hillside to explore the Eugenia Mine ruins. Glide northeast from the tumble-down log cabin, dropping slowly through tall, black-barked lodgepole pine. Continue through an open glen, cross a shallow drainage, and follow the trail through deer-scarred aspen. Pass several fire-blackened pitch stumps and break into wide Moore Park. Return over the ski tracks.

Making friends with a gray jay

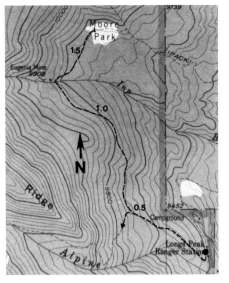

28 MILLS AND BLACK LAKES

One day trip
Classification: Intermediate to Advanced
Distance: 3.7 miles one way
Skiing time: 3-3½ hours one way
Elevation gain: 1,360 feet
Maximum elevation: 10,640 feet
Season: December through April
Topographic map:
   U.S.G.S. McHenrys Peak, Colo. 7.5'

Breath-taking scenery and tremendous down-hill skiing are chief motivations for a tour to Mills and Black Lakes. Viewed from the north rim of Black Lake, Longs Peak, highest in the Estes Park area, crests at 14,255 feet behind a row of jagged spires, appropriately called the Keyboard of the Winds. Pagoda Mountain and Chiefs Head Peak south combine to form a vast and barren amphitheater which encompasses the high Green and Frozen Lakes. The Spear-head, north of the amphitheater wall, points skyward and Arrowhead mountain west forms a huge granite fortress. Contour lines on the topo map delineate the obvious rationale for these latter two toponyms.

From Beaver Meadows entrance station to Rocky Mountain National Park drive 0.2 mile farther west, then turn south on the Bear Lake and Moraine Park road. Stay on this main road another 8.1 miles to Glacier Gorge Junction, identified by a sign on the right side of the road. A parking area inside the hairpin turn is kept open throughout the winter.

Cross the road to a bulletin board posted with Park regulations and weather informa-tion. Begin skiing south on the trail, soon passing a sign with summer trail mileages. Maintain elevation, taking the southeast trail to Mills Lake as a trail fork drops east to Glacier Basin. The trail rises slightly, then descends to a creek drainage. Foot travel packs the trail along these first few hundred yards, necessitating some herringbone or sidestep for the short climbs; soon however only ski and snowshoe tracks mark the snow.

Cross the small creek on an old log bridge and turn up the drainage, leaving the summer trail. Stay south of the creekbed and rocky hillside and climb through willows and spruce. Soon the trail heads southwest toward the silhouetted "thumb" on Otis Peak. Glide over several icy beaver ponds, swing south through the Glacier Knobs, and glide through a flat, well-forested area. Ski along the west Glacier Knob mountainside, pass the Loch Vale ravine (No. 29), and head southwest toward Glacier Gorge. Stay west of Glacier Creek to large Mills Lake, avoiding a road-like cul-de-sac up Thatchtop Mountain.

Glide to the southeast side of the lake and climb south over a slight rise to Jewel Lake. Continue south between Thatchtop and the Storm Peak range on an easy climb up Glacier Gorge; break from the englemann spruce and switchback a series of giant snow steps to a viewpoint on the high north rim of Black Lake. These steps make exciting downhill shusses on the return trip which takes only half the time as the trip in.

Below Black Lake

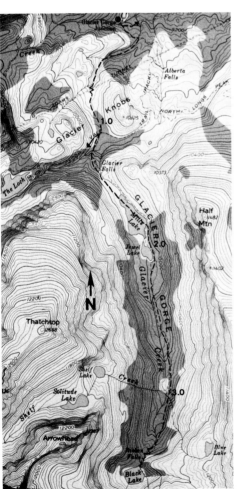

29 THE LOCH AND TIMBERLINE FALLS

One day trip
Classification: Advanced
Distance: 2.4 miles one way
Skiing time: 2-2½ hours one way
Elevation gain: 1,160 feet
Maximum elevation: 10,440 feet
Season: December through April
Topographic map:
  U.S.G.S. McHenrys Peak, Colo. 7.5'

Cold winter wind whips down Taylor Peak and continues unabated through the wide ravine of Loch Vale. The Loch itself, named after the Scottish word for lake, freezes into rounded, undulating waves. With the aid of an opened parka or ground cloth the tourer can sail on a quick but leg-shaking and unstable ride across the lake. A downhill shuss through a series of giant steps in Loch Vale ranks as another chief delight of the tour.

Winter temperatures stop the splash of Icy Brook over Timberline Falls. With a short but steep hike up the quiet Falls mountainside an adventurous tourer can extend the tour to Glass Lake and Sky Pond, seldom seen until summer. This additional effort affords an excellent view of The Sharkstooth spire, precipitous Taylor Peak, and the steep-walled cirque containing Taylor Glacier. Weather conditions are best for this trip in late April.

Drive through the Beaver Meadows entrance station into Rocky Mountain National Park and take the south turn 0.2 mile farther west to Bear Lake and Moraine Park. Continue another 8.1 miles on the main road to Glacier Gorge Junction, identified by a sign on the right side of the road. A parking area inside the hairpin turn is plowed out through the winter.

Begin skiing south from the bulletin board across the road from the parking area, soon passing a sign with summer trail mileages. Turn southeast on the Mills Lake summer trail when a fork drops east to Glacier Basin. Climb slightly on the hillside, then descend to the drainage bottom. Foot travel is common along these first few hundred yards, requiring herringbone or sidestep through the packed, crusty snow; soon however only ski and snowshoe tracks appear.

Ski over the bridge and turn up the drainage, leaving the summer trail. Stay south of the creekbed and rocky hillside and climb through the willows and englemann spruce. As the trail heads southwest a curious "thumb" on Otis Peak becomes silhouetted against the sky. Glide over several icy beaver ponds, swing south through the Glacier Knobs, and glide over a flat, well-forested area. Skirt the east side of west Glacier Knob to the wide Loch Vale; climb up the steep-sided valley on the north side of Icy Brook. The trail winds through tall fir and spruce, then breaks clear of trees into a wide, white-walled ravine. Sheer granite walls of Glacier Knobs crowd into the vale overhead.

Switchback the steep snow-steps below The Loch and continue west to the lake. Limber pine, characteristic of windy areas in the subalpine zone, appear on the rocky mountainside. Cross to the southwest side of the lake and continue up the Icy Brook drainage. A treeless snow lane south of Icy Brook makes a good route for the first half mile. Curve south with the drainage until the steep, boulder-covered Timberline Falls blocks further progress. If weather permits cross to far west side of the vale and pick a route up the mountainside, continuing to Glass Lake and Sky Pond. Return over the ski tracks.

Frozen waves of the Loch

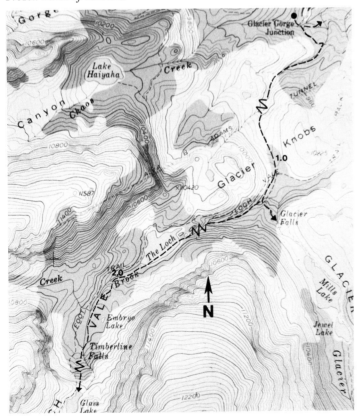

30 NYMPH, DREAM, AND EMERALD LAKES

Half-day trip
Classification: Beginner or Intermediate
Distance: 1.8 miles one way
Skiing time: 1½-2 hours one way
Elevation gain: 660 feet
Maximum elevation: 10,120 feet
Season: Mid-December through April
Topographic map:
  U.S.G.S. McHenrys Peak, Colo. 7.5'

Do beautiful maidens dwell in secluded pine bowers around Nymph Lake? Rocky Mountain National Park did have a lovely nature child at one time. Clad in a leopard skin she lived in the wilds on pine bark soup, mountain trout, and wild honey. But, alas! That was in days gone by: a publicity stunt in 1917 staged by the Park Superintendent with the help of an attractive assistant. Actually Nymph Lake was named after the yellow pond lily, once-called Nymphae Polysepala, that graces the lake in summer.

Encircled by conifers, snow-covered Nymph Lake makes an easy destination point for the beginning skier. For more experienced skiers the tricky climb over the ridge west brings to view the elongated bowl of Dream Lake; an easier climb up Tyndall Gorge ends at the vast glacial bowl of Emerald Lake. If avalanche danger is low, climb the smooth mountainside immediately west of Emerald Lake for a powder run of linked turns to the lake bottom.

Drive through the Beaver Meadows entrance station into Rocky Mountain National Park; turn south after 0.2 mile to Bear Lake and Moraine Park. Proceed on the main road another 9.1 miles, continuing past Glacier Gorge Junction to the large Bear Lake parking lot.

An elaborate Information Station across the road west illustrates summer trails and lakes. A view from Bear Lake, immediately over the rise northwest, offers a preliminary look at the steep ridge and general trail area between Nymph and Dream Lakes. Intersect the summer trail to Nymph Lake by skiing west from the Information Station, then follow the trail south soon passing the log Ranger Station cabin. Maintain elevation and turn southwest on the obscure trail when a branch fork drops southeast to Glacier Gorge Junction. Climb gradually through sheltering lodgepole pine on the knoll east of Nymph Lake. An occasional glimpse southwest through the trees reveals the Chaos Creek drainage and Hallet Peak range.

Continue on the summer trail southwest then west to Nymph Lake. From the south edge take a compass reading west and locate a landmark on the ridgetop. This landmark, in approximate line with Dream Lake, will serve as a trail guide for the switchback climb between the two lakes. Cross to the northwest side of Nymph Lake, leaving the summer trail, and climb several hundred yards through the trees. Switchback west up the hillside, avoiding the steep avalanche paths; then cross over a rise south to the landmark. Turn west and make the gradual climb to Dream Lake.

From Dream Lake contour west up the south side of Tyndall Gorge to a rise covered with large boulders. Cross to the north side of the gorge and continue the climb to Emerald Lake. On the return trip ski down the creekbed from Emerald Lake to Dream Lake, then proceed over the ski tracks.

Below Emerald Lake

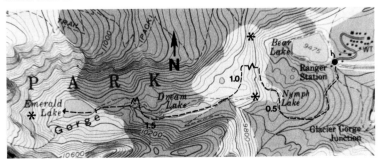

31 GLACIER CREEK TRAIL

One day trip
Classification: Beginner
Distance: 4.4 miles one way
Skiing time: 2½-3 hours one way
Elevation *loss*: 880 feet
Maximum elevation: 9,480 feet
Season: January through February
Topographic maps:
    U.S.G.S. McHenrys Peak, Colo. 7.5′
    U.S.G.S. Longs Peak, Colo. 7.5′

The Glacier Creek Trail with a starting point at Bear Lake offers a delightful change from most Front Range ski tours: it follows a downhill route! The trail, clearly defined with red arrowhead markers, begins with a quick drop to Glacier Gorge Junction, then descends more gradually to Glacier Basin. After winding through Prospect Canyon the route, now flat and easy gliding, circumvents the Sprague Lake area and continues through the "C" loop of Glacier Basin Campground. The tour requires a drop-off car at Bear Lake and a pick-up car at Glacier Basin Campground turn-off.

Drive through the Beaver Meadows entrance station into Rocky Mountain National Park. Soon turn south to Bear Lake and Moraine Park and pass the tour stopping point at the Glacier Basin Campground turnoff, another 5.3 miles. Continue to a large parking area at the end of the Bear Lake Road.

An Information Station at the far west end of the parking area marks the trailhead. Ski a few yards west from this sign to intersect the trail to Glacier Basin Campground. Follow the trail south, immediately crossing an inconspicuous branch of Glacier Creek, pass left of the log cabin Ranger Station. Take the left fork where a branch trail forks to Nymph Lake (No. 30) and drop quickly southeast. Continue in and out of lodgepole pine and fir to Glacier Gorge Junction.

Follow the trail over a small rise, cross the bridge over Chaos Creek, and fork left where another trail turns right to Mills and Black Lakes (No. 28) and The Loch and Timberline Falls (No. 29). Glide east on the level trail passing under a mountainside of big boulders and ski over Glacier Creek on the snow-filled footbridge. Continue down the aspen and lodgepole pine covered mountainside to the bottom of Glacier Basin. Curve around the frozen pond in Prospect Canyon, then head northeast on the shaded, winding trail.

After a long section of easy gliding, begin a very slight uphill climb. Continue straight as Boulder Brook Trail turns south, cross two branches of Boulder Brook, and traverse the mountainside. Continue on the left fork where the Storm Pass Trail turns more steeply up the hillside and eventually ski out of the lodgepole pine to a spectacular vista west. The range from high Taylor Peak curves down to round-topped, steep-sided Otis Peak and a broad saddle spans the gap to the sharper Hallet Peak. A granite-ribbed cirque forms the west wall of Tyndall Gorge and connects Hallet Peak with Flattop Mountain. Notchtop Mountain and Knobtop Mountain can be identified farther north.

Continue back into the trees on the winding trail, pass a northeast fork to the YMCA area, and intersect the "C" loop of Glacier Basin Campground. Follow the wide road to a wind-blown meadow and continue across the bridge over the much larger Glacier Creek to the second parking area.

Information station near Bear Lake

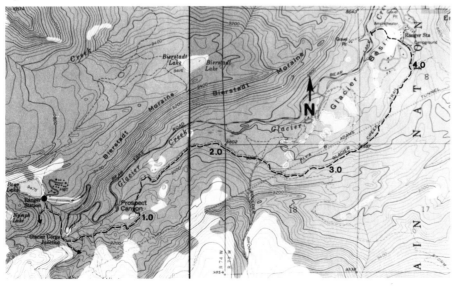

32 SPRAGUE LAKE

Half-day trip
Classification: Beginner
Distance: 1.9 miles one way
Skiing time: 1-1½ hours one way
Elevation gain: 220 feet
Maximum elevation: 8,800 feet
Season: January through February
Topographic map:
  U.S.G.S. Longs Peak, Colo. 7.5'

A maze of flat, interconnected trails weaves through the lodgepole pine near Sprague Lake, making this area a favorite among ski tourers. Lower elevation shortens the general season but trails again become skiable after each snow in March and early April.

Drive through the Beaver Meadows entrance station into Rocky Mountain National Park. Turn south after 0.2 mile on the Bear Lake Road and continue another 5.3 miles to the Glacier Basin Campground turnoff. Park on the closed Glacier Basin Campground road near the yellow pipe gate and bridge.

Begin skiing from the highway bridge over Glacier Creek; drop to the west side of the creekbed and glide south through the deeper snow in the lodgepole pine. Continue a cross-country course paralleling the creekbed. Swing near Bear Lake Road and soon cross the drainage south where a north branch fork joins Glacier Creek. Make a short climb through willows and pine to a series of snow-covered beaver ponds. From these open areas rounded peaks come to view: Emerald Mountain lies northeast and Gianttrack Mountain, named from a legendary finding by Arapahos of gigantic human footprints, rises beyond on the horizon. Rams Horn Mountain and Lily Mountain complete the forested panorama.

Ski cross-country south linking the icy beaver ponds. Pass through a stand of dead timber, follow the creekbed southwest through lodgepole pine, and ski into the south end of a large meadow, the site of a lake until the dam gave way in 1970. Climb a small rise east of Sprague Lake and follow a path around the north side. Warmer temperatures at the lower 8,700 foot elevation usually make Sprague Lake unsafe for crossing.

Ski west from Sprague Lake, pass the Glacier Livery barn and corral area, and continue to the west end of an oval parking area. Turn south past a steep trail that follows the north fork of Glacier Creek and climb on a trail above the beaver pond willows. The trail proceeds southwest, levels through shaded, black-trunked lodgepole pine, and continues past two branch trails which join the Glacier Creek Trail.

Glide downhill northwest and west, cross Glacier Creek on a large log footbridge, and, after a very easy climb, enter an open meadow. A scenic view west of jagged Otis, Hallett, and Flattop Mountains makes this spot a good place for lunch and relaxation. Return over the ski tracks or via a loop tour on Glacier Creek Trail (No. 31).

Oops

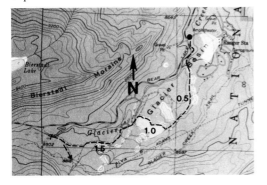

33 BIERSTADT LAKE

Half-day trip
Classification: Beginner to Intermediate
Distance: 1.9 miles one way
Skiing time: 1-1½ hours one way
Elevation gain: 340 feet
Maximum elevation: 9,760 feet
Season: Mid-December through mid-April
Topographic map:
   U.S.G.S. McHenrys Peak, Colo. 7.5'

A vista of rugged mountain peaks greets the tourer on the open climb up Bierstadt Moraine but soon the trail lies hidden in a shady, silent forest of towering conifers. After leaving the well-marked Mill Creek Basin trail, the route to Bierstadt Lake becomes increasingly harder to distinguish among the tall conifers and the tourer must depend upon a compass and good sense of distance for a cross-country course. However, the wide, snow-covered lake makes a target that is hard to miss.

Drive through the Beaver Meadows entrance station into Rocky Mountain National Park; turn south after 0.2 mile to Bear Lake and Moraine Park. Proceed on the main road another 9.1 miles, continuing past Glacier Gorge Junction to the large Bear Lake parking lot.

An Information Station at the west end of the parking lot provides orientation of lakes and summer trails in the area. Begin skiing northwest from this sign toward Bear Lake; cross above the east end of the lake and follow red arrowhead trail markers north past a small boulder field and through an aspen grove. Traverse the Bierstadt Moraine mountainside northeast, soon gaining a good view of the surrounding snow-capped peaks. Across wide Glacier Basin the steep, glacial-carved west side of Half Mountain contrasts sharply with the gently arcing east side. The Storm Peak ridgetop stretches south toward the pointed spires of the Keyboard of the Winds; Pagoda Mountain, Chiefs Head Peak, and McHenrys Peak form an enormous cirque west of the Keyboard of the Winds. The east face of Longs Peak, vast and imposing even from a distance of five miles, rises above Mount Lady Washington south-southeast.

Continue the steady uphill climb, keeping right when a branch trail switchbacks left to Lake Helene (No. 35) and Odessa and Fern Lakes (No. 36). Ski over the Bierstadt Moraine ridgetop, turn northwest, and glide on a gentle downhill drop into lodgepole pine. Soon turn northeast again and follow the trail markers on a steady downhill drop. The shaded trail descends gradually to the snow-filled basin floor, then winds through tall fir and spruce.

Weave through reddish-brown fir trunks on a flat trail. As the Mill Creek Basin trail continues straight, fork right onto the Bierstadt Lake trail, marked by a half-buried sign. Glide over the level trail and soon begin a gradual but steady descent. Pass through a section of dead standing timber mixed with the lodgepole pine and curve northeast through a small, snow-filled glen. As the trail becomes difficult to follow, take a compass reading for orientation and proceed east-northeast on a cross-country course to Bierstadt Lake, staying well north of the steep Bierstadt Moraine mountainside. The panorama of mountain peaks south and southeast can again be seen from the open, snowy lakebed. Return over the ski tracks or follow a more northerly alternate route, intercepting the Mill Creek Basin trail farther down the mountainside, then climbing steeply southwest.

Bierstadt Lake

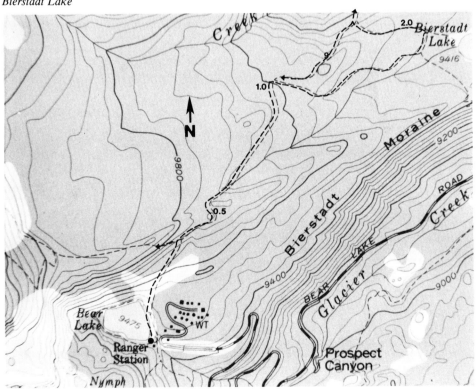

34 MILL CREEK BASIN

One day trip
Classification: Intermediate
Distance: 4.2 miles one way
Skiing time: 2-2½ hours one way
Elevation gain: 260 feet
Maximum elevation: 9,740 feet
Season: Mid-December through March
Topographic maps:
U.S.G.S. McHenrys Peak, Colo. 7.5'
U.S.G.S. Longs Peak, Colo. 7.5'

The trail from Bear Lake to the Hallowell Park turnoff measures 4.2 miles but the tour takes only about two hours if snow conditions are fast. After an initial climb up the Bierstadt Moraine mountainside, the shaded path, clearly defined with red arrowhead trail markers, winds through a forest of tall conifers, then drops steeply to Mill Creek Basin. The unprotected road through Hallowell Park often is wind-scoured, necessitating a short hike to the parking area. The tour requires a drop-off car at Bear Lake parking lot and a pick-up car at Hallowell Park turnoff.

Drive through the Beaver Meadows entrance station into Rocky Mountain National Park. Soon turn south onto the Bear Lake Road and proceed 3.6 miles to the Hallowell Park turnoff. Park one car near the end of the Hallowell Park road, then continue another 5.5 miles in a second car to the large Bear Lake parking lot.

Being skiing northwest from the "Information Station" sign at the west end of the parking lot. Cross above the east end of Bear Lake, pass a small boulder field, and follow the red arrowhead trail markers through an aspen grove. Climb northwest up the Bierstadt Moraine mountainside to a good view of the surrounding mountains, and pass the branch trail to Lake Helene (No. 35) and Odessa and Fern Lakes (No. 36). Ski over the ridgetop, turn northwest, and glide down a slight drop into the lodgepole pine. After another turn northeast, well-marked by arrowhead markers, the trail drops steadily down the north side of the ridge.

Glide past tall fir and spruce and continue on the shaded trail into a climax forest. Fir trees block all landmarks but the conspicuous trail gives no orienteering problems. Stay left where a branch trail turns right to Bierstadt Lake and follow the arrowhead markers to a steep, north-facing hillside. Here a strong snowplow and fast step turns are useful as the trail plunges like a bobsled run toward Mill Creek Basin northeast.

Pass an uphill fork to Bierstadt Lake, and soon begin a more gradual drop through rust-colored pine trunks. Curve west on a steep descent to Mill Creek, then follow the trail along the east side of the creekbed. At Mill Creek Basin the trail turns east, passes by a rocky knoll in front of Steep Mountain, and breaks into an open meadow. Wind northwest through a grove of tall, deer-scarred aspen, cross the footbridge over Mill Creek, and proceed under the granite outcroppings north to the windy, spacious Hallowell Park. Hike over the wind-scoured road to the parking area.

Beaver lodge on Mill Creek

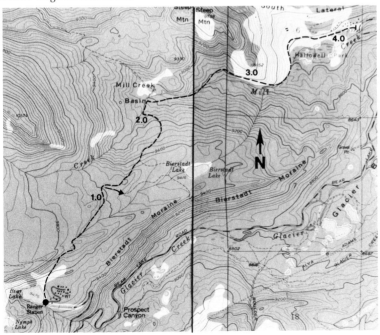

35 LAKE HELENE

One day trip
Classification: Beginner to Intermediate
Distance: 2.8 miles one way
Skiing time: 2½-3 hours one way
Elevation gain: 1,120 feet
Maximum elevation: 10,600 feet
Season: Mid-December through mid-April
Topographic map:
  U.S.G.S. McHenrys Peak, Colo. 7.5'

A vast snowfield crossing and a scenic vantage point highlight the tour to Lake Helene. From the north rim of the lake the steep-sided Fern Creek Valley falls steeply, girded by Joe Mills Mountain east, Knobtop and Little Matterhorn mountains west. Notchtop Mountain, a vast granite monolith topped with a unique gap, stands immediately west. The tour traverses the open northeast side of Flattop Mountain, following closely the summer trail that lies buried under many feet of snow. After new snow, when avalanche danger is high, follow a course with tree protection lower down the mountainside.

Drive through the Beaver Meadows entrance station into Rocky Mountain National Park; turn south after 0.2 mile on the road to Bear Lake and Moraine Park. Proceed another 9.1 miles to the large Bear Lake parking lot, passing Glacier Gorge Junction.

An Information Station across the road west provides a good diagram of the lakes and summer trails near Bear Lake. Begin skiing northwest from this Information Station, cross above the east end of Bear Lake, and follow the red arrowhead trail markers north past a small boulder field and through a small aspen grove. Begin the climb up Bierstadt Moraine, gaining elevation for a good look at wide Glacier Basin southeast and the distinctive cirque area near Black Lake south. The flat top and sheer east face of 14,255 foot Longs Peak soars above Mount Lady Washington south-southeast. A sign near the Bierstadt Moraine ridgetop signals a switchback turn southwest onto the Fern Lake trail; the northeast fork continues to Bierstadt Lake (No. 33) and Mill Creek (No. 34).

Stay high on the ridgetop through englemann spruce and lodgepole pine; cross to the north side and continue west staying about 100 feet under the ridgetop. Through the trees Mount Wuh, named after the Arapahoe word for grizzly bear, shapes the north side of the Mill Creek drainage. Pass the fork up steep Flattop Mountain west, cross a small drainage, bend northwest and begin a gradual climb. Soon the white, snow patch of Bierstadt Lake becomes visible east.

Break out of the scattered limber pine and continue the climb northwest, staying high on the mountainside and crossing the open snowfield. Turn west into the trees as the Mill Creek drainage falls away north, and maintain elevation to the creek basin. Pass a sign with summer trail mileages and follow the drainage to Marigold Pond and Two Rivers Lake. Continue southwest to Lake Helene, cross to the north end, and ski up over the lip to a good viewpoint and lunch spot. Return over the ski tracks.

Snowfield crossing to Lake Helene

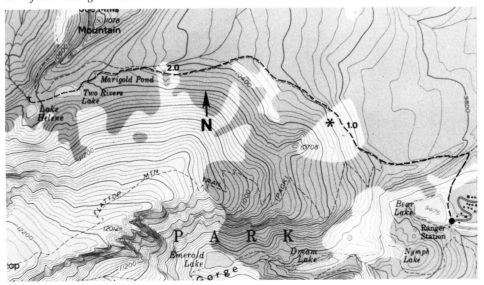

36 ODESSA AND FERN LAKES

One day trip or overnight
Classification: Advanced
Distance: 10.6 miles one way
Skiing time: 5-5½ hours one way
Elevation gain: 2,580 feet
Maximum elevation: 10,600 feet
Season: Mid-December through March
Topographic maps:
   U.S.G.S. McHenrys Peak, Colo. 7.5'
   U.S.G.S. Longs Peak, Colo. 7.5'

In 1916, ski aficionados of the Colorado Mountain Club joined the Estes Park Outdoor Club for the first "snow frolic" at Fern Lake Lodge. No packed slopes or ski lifts here! The winter adventurers managed the uphill trip on snowshoes, pulling their heavy, wooden skis behind them. In later years club members bound their skis with rope to walk uphill and eventually learned the art of turning skis on the downhill run from an Italian army officer ($1 a lesson). Today the area around Fern Lake still offers exceptional skiing. From Bear Lake the tour route loops high into the sub-alpine zone to Lake Helene, then plummets down the Fern Creek valley and continues to Moraine Park. The trip can be done fairly easily in one day but an overnight camp allows time for an extra run or two through the snowfields above Odessa Lake. (See the Introduction for regulations concerning overnight camping in Rocky Mountain National Park).

Drive through the Beaver Meadows entrance station into Rocky Mountain National Park. Turn south after 0.2 miles onto the Bear Lake Road and proceed to the Moraine Park access road, marked by a sign. Turn west and drive as far as possible into Moraine Park. Leave one car here, then continue in a second car to the large Bear Lake parking lot.

From the "Information Station" at the west end of the parking lot ski northwest over a small rise toward Bear Lake. Like most lakes in Rocky Mountain National Park, Bear Lake was formed by the powerful scooping action of a massive glacier. The displaced soil and rock debris can be seen on each side of the lake basin, forming long ridges called lateral moraines. Look west across the snowy lakebed to the skyline for a view of the sheer cliff of Hallett Peak, the saddle of Tyndall Gorge, and the bald top of Flattop Mountain.

Weave through the scattered conifers above the east end of Bear Lake, then follow the red arrowhead markers past a boulder field and through a small aspen grove. Begin a steady climb northeast up the Bierstadt Moraine mountainside and soon gain a superb view of the forested Glacier Basin and surrounding rocky peaks. Directly south, the two, rounded Glacier Knobs can be seen on either side of the entry way to deep Glacier Gorge. On the east side of the gorge is glacial-torn Half Mountain, still covered with blackened trunks from a fire in 1900; on the west side is Thatchtop Mountain, shaped like a huge loaf of bread. The horizon south-southeast exposes the monolithic east face of Longs Peak rising above nearby

The telemark turn

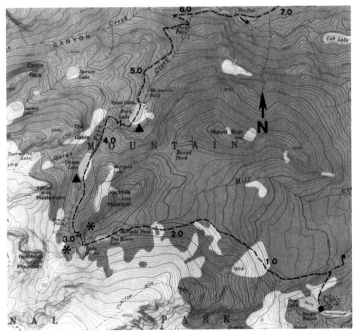

Pagoda Mountain and Chiefs Head Peak.

Turn sharply southwest onto the Fern Lake trail before reaching the Bierstadt Moraine ridgetop, leaving the marked trail to Bierstadt Lake (No. 33) and Mill Creek Basin (No. 34). The sign which marks the turn may be covered with snow but the trail is a conspicuous uphill path. Climb to the ridgetop, then cross-country west along the north side of the ridge. Through the trees north the long, forested Mount Wuh, named after the Arapaho word for grizzly bear, stretches along the far side of the Mills Creek drainage.

Ski west toward Flattop Mountain until the mountainside starts to rise, then bend northwest and begin a gentle uphill contour. Soon the white patch of Bierstadt Lake can be spotted in the middle of the forested ridge east. Gradually leave the tree cover and with the twin summits of Stones Peak as the northwest bearing, break trail across an open, windswept snowfield. After a new snow when avalanche danger is high, follow a safer course through the trees lower on the mountainside.

Curve west as the Mill Creek drainage falls away north and maintain elevation to the creek basin. Pass a sign with summer trail mileages and follow the drainage past snow-covered Marigold Pond and icy Two Rivers Lake. Then, with the deep cirque under Ptarmigan Point as the next bearing, continue to Lake Helene. Here the tourer has a close-up look at the snow-crusted, granite face of Notchtop

Mountain west. Climb over the north lip of the Lake Helene basin and negotiate a cross-country course down the steep mountainside with long, sweeping telemark turns, avoiding avalanche danger farther west. Glide down one open snowfield after another in an exhilerating descent through the Fern Creek valley to Odessa Lake.

In the inlet to Odessa Lake pools of water remain open all winter, making this south end a logical overnight campsite. On the trip to Fern Lake stay in the smooth bed of Fern Creek until the hillside begins to drop east, then follow the natural slope of the hill to the lake basin. Thick trees on the more protected south side create another excellent overnight camping spot. Be sure to take time to explore the old Fern Lake Lodge at the northeast side of the lake. Built in 1910, the Lodge soon made the area a well-known beauty spot. The living room floor of the Lodge was ingeniously constructed of cross sections of logs which still remain today.

Pick up the summer trail at the north end of Fern Lake and follow the switchbacks down to the pool. Snow-shoe and boot travel pack the snow on this steep, narrow trail, creating a fast, challenging run. From the pool choose a route over the flat summer trail or the icy beaver ponds in the Big Thompson River; proceed east to the picnic grounds and continue over the windswept roadbed through Moraine Park to the parking area.

Odessa Lake

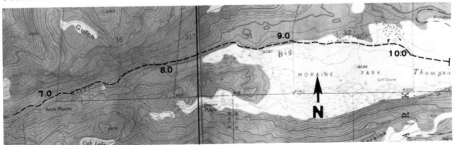

37 BEAVER MEADOWS

Half-day trip
Classification: Beginner
Distance: 4.0 miles round trip
Skiing time: 2-2½ hours round trip
Elevation gain: 380 feet
Maximum elevation: 8,680 feet
Season: January through March
Topographic maps:
 U.S.G.S. Longs Peak, Colo. 7.5′
 U.S.G.S. Estes Park, Colo. 7.5′

Scattered ponderosa pine surround Beaver Meadows but most of the area around Beaver Creek is an open, rolling snow field. The perfect "ski-baseball" field for a crowd of skiers, Beaver Meadows also provides a quiet, rewarding nature trek for the lone tourer. Despite the toponymic enchantment with beavers, none live atop Beaver Mountain west of Beaver Meadows, apparently named by association with Beaver Brook. In fact, little evidence of beaver dams, lodges, or ponds can be found along Beaver Brook in Beaver Meadows. The little park is, however, a winter haven for elk, deer, and snowshoe hares.

Lower elevation plus wind and sun exposure create inconstant snow conditions in Beaver Meadows and even in midwinter months the park will sometimes be bare of snow. After a period of recent snowfall, however, the loop tour never fails to make a pleasant winter outing.

Drive through the Beaver Meadows entrance station to Rocky Mountain National Park, pass the south fork to Bear Lake and Moraine Park, and curve north 0.8 mile to the Beaver Meadows turnout on the west side of the road. Park at the turnout or off the paved road.

Climb through the gate across Beaver Meadows access road and begin skiing west, staying north of Beaver Brook. Usually the drifted jeep road makes the best route through the dense sagebrush. Leave the jeep road when it swings south and follow a summer pack trail northwest toward Deer Ridge. Wind cross-country up the drainage through scattered aspen. Deer and elk often hide in the brush near the creekbed, fleeing into thicker timber at the least sound.

Cross the creekbed when the climb becomes too steep and glide cross-country down the west side. Soon contour south out of the drainage, picking an easy route through the scattered ponderosa pines. Climb a gentle rise then glide over the rolling hillside toward Beaver Brook. Before breaking from tree cover, scan the meadow for wildlife. The thick willows in Beaver Brook are another excellent place to spot deer and elk.

Continue past a chain-fenced filtration plant and picnic area. Swing east and intercept a summer trail, then climb gradually back into ponderosa pine. Glide along the obscure trail to the open meadowland, cross the Beaver Brook drainage, and continue to the parking area.

86

Elk in Beaver Meadows

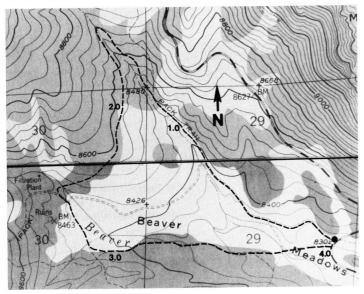

38 FALL RIVER ROAD

Overnight
Classification: Advanced
Distance: 9.8 miles one way
Skiing time: 5-5½ hours one way
Elevation gain: 2,810 feet
Maximum elevation: 11,440 feet
Season: Mid-December through April
Topographic map:
    U.S.G.S. Trail Ridge, Colo. 7.5'

Many conditions that make an excellent ski tour come together in the overnight trip to Willow Park. The tour route follows Fall River Road through an area rich in history and interesting geomorphology, then drops on a thrilling, mile-long downhill run to Willow Park. When fresh powder covers these high, wind-packed snow fields, the ski tourer can float effortlessly through long, arcing turns and short wedels. Plan the trip after a new snowfall because Fall River Road can be windswept several miles above Chasm Falls. Pack in plenty of water and prepare for the wintry conditions above Willow Park even if it feels like spring in Horseshoe Park. (See the Introduction for regulations concerning camping in Rocky Mountain National Park).

Drive through the Fall River entrance station into Rocky Mountain National Park and proceed on the Trail Ridge Road another 2.1 miles to the junction with Fall River Road. Turn north and continue to the end of the plowed road, usually near the parking area for the Lawn Lake Trailhead

Begin skiing northwest then west on Fall River Road; soon glide through an elk-and-deer scarred aspen grove and pass south of an old log cabin. In 1913-14 this cabin and others nearby housed "Tom Tynan's boys," convicts from the Colorado Penitentiary who made up the pick-and-shovel road gang for beginning construction of Fall River Road. Proceed along the north side of Horseshoe Park toward Endovalley Campground.

Turn right past the access loop to Endovalley Campground, pass through a yellow gate, and begin a moderate climb above the valley floor. A glance toward the thickly forested mountainside south shows the long, white cuts of Trail Ridge Road, the famous "wonder road" that replaced steep Fall River Road in 1932. Cross the bridge over Chiquita Creek and glide west through the narrowing valley. After a climb through two switchbacks, the rounded, bald top of Specimen Mountain comes into view on the horizon west. The Arapaho Indians spoke of this mountain as "Mountain Smokes" and geologists have found that the mountain did indeed send up smoke — a volcano which erupted millions of years ago. Continue the gradual climb west to Chasm Falls, a good rest and lunch spot. Sharply pointed spires, sculptured by the expansion and contraction of frost-wedging, jut into the sky on the ridgetop north. Follow the roadcut as it hugs the steep valley wall, then breaks into a level clearing. From 1908 to 1940 this clearing was the "terri-

Snow cave

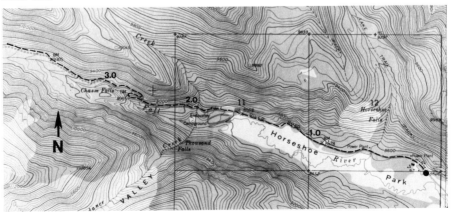

89

tory" of miner Bill Currance. Paying little heed to the establishment of Rocky Mountain National Park, "Crazy Bill" lived alone in his isolated cabin and with a shotgun defended his territorial right against trespassers. Every morning the miner could watch the first rays of sunlight flicker from the rocky peak south so he called it Sundance Mountain.

Wind through a switchback and continue the steady climb west over the roadbed. Look south for beautiful cascades of blue ice that form from run-off water on Sundance Mountain. Climb through a series of long, winding switchbacks on the south side of Mount Chapin. Handbuilt rock retaining walls supported these steep switchbacks in the 1920's and hours of hand labor were required to repair the terraces each spring. After a cloudburst washed out the switchbacks in July 1953, the road was closed until 1968. Today wire mesh baskets filled with rocks stabilize these landslide areas. Be alert for a snowslide near the last switchback especially after a new snow. Fan Slide catches the corner of the switchback and spreads to the lower road; Old Faithful Slide, named after running each day between 2 and 3 p.m. for thirteen consecutive days, covers the road a few hundred feet farther west.

Swing northwest as Fall Creek rises near the road again, pass a tributary creek in the narrow cut of Canoncito or "little canyon," and soon break out into long, Willow Park.

Continue on a northwest roadcut to the Willow Park Patrol Cabin. Originally built in 1924 for road maintenance crews, this picturesque log shelter later served pre-lift ski enthusiasts as a base for skiing the Fall River Basin. For the overnight camp, pitch a tent in the thick stands of englemann spruce on the valley floor or dig a snow cave in the deeply drifted switchbacks above the park.

Follow Fall River Road through four winding switchbacks in the next mile, climbing high up the north moraine mountainside. Curve past the deep ravine of Chapin Pass, continue the steady climb northwest, and soon enter the winter world of the alpine life zone. Here "tree islands" of scrubby fir and juniper struggle against the high wind and frigid temperatures of a climate quite similar to that beyond the Arctic Circle. Inspect the mountainside carefully for a rare glimpse of a white-tailed ptarmigan in its camouflaged winter plumage. Cross-country west until the moraine wall becomes less steep, then drop into the basin and downhill through vast, open snow fields to Willow Park.

A winter shelter

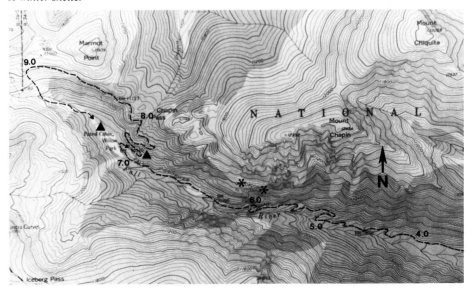

39 LAWN LAKE

One day trip
Classification: Intermediate to Advanced
Distance: 5.8 miles one way
Skiing time: 4½-5 hours one way
Elevation gain: 2,460 feet
Maximum elevation: 11,000 feet
Season: Mid-December through mid-April
Topographic maps:
   U.S.G.S. Trail Ridge, Colo. 7.5′
   U.S.G.S. Estes Park, Colo. 7.5′

The steep southern reaches of Bighorn Mountain present an immediate obstacle in the Lawn Lake tour but after the first, often snow-bare switchbacks, a delightfully easy trail meanders north through the secluded Roaring River Valley. Near the 3.0 mile mark the trail resumes an exhilerating switchback climb, reaching an altitude of 11,000 feet at Lawn Lake. Here Hagues Peak (northwest), fourth highest in Rocky Mountain National Park, and Fairchild

Mountain (west) dominate the panorama. A rugged, glacial cirque containing unseen Crystal Lake carves a steep-walled bowl into the east side of Fairchild Mountain. Be prepared for bad weather at Lawn Lake: temperatures range 10° to 20° F. colder than the trailhead temperature; wind speed increases two to three times.

Drive through the Fall River entrance station into Rocky Mountain National Park; proceed on the Trail Ridge Road another 2.1 miles to the junction with Fall River Road. Turn north and continue less than 0.1 mile to a parking area for the Lawn Lake trailhead.

Pack skis north to the summer trailhead, passing a bulletin board with Park regulations and general weather information. Herringbone and sidestep the terraced trail on a switchback climb up the hillside, join the horse trail, and ski into the sheltering fir and ponderosa pine. From the higher vantage point a look south encompasses much of crooked Fall River in the long Horseshoe Park. Across the park white ribbons of Trail Ridge Road contrast sharply with the green Hidden Valley mountainside.

Climb northwest toward the winter-stilled Roaring River, then soon drop slightly into the snowy basin. Glide north in and out of sunny, open patches, staying east of the Roaring River. Cross through a grove of lodgepole pine, swing closer to the river, and pass the Upsilon Lake trail. Soon the white, rounded peaks of Fairchild and Mummy Mountains are visible north on the horizon. Cross through a windfall area, glide through an aspen grove, then follow the blazes back into the trees. Here wind can roar through the treetops but leave the trail unscathed.

Turn east from the Roaring River near the 3.0 mile mark and make the switchback climb through scattered limber pine up Bighorn Mountain. Traverse the exposed mountainside through windpacked, crusty snow and ski up another series of tight switchbacks under the rocky Mummy Mountain. Scattered pitch trunks along the trail, remnants of a forest fire, stick through the snow on the barren slope.

Swing west at the steep south wall of Mummy Mountain; break into an open park and cross-country through deep snow on the north side of the Roaring River drainage. Continue onto the wind-hardened snow of Lawn Lake's lee side and ski up a small rise to the lake. For the return trip retrace the ski tracks on the summer trail. A return down the Roaring Fork drainage begins well but soon becomes cluttered with rocks and trees.

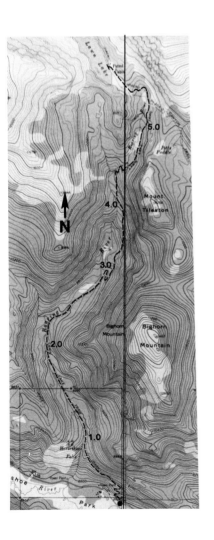

Skiing into the wind near Lawn Lake

40 PENNOCK PASS

One day trip
Classification: Beginner to Advanced
Distance: 3.0 miles one way
Skiing time: 1½-2 hours one way
Elevation gain: 900 feet
Maximum elevation: 9,200 feet
Season: January through mid-March
Topographic map:
   U.S.G.S. Pingree Park, Colo. 7.5′

Stands of tall lodgepole pine shade the smooth Pennock Pass Road and create good snow conditions despite the low elevation. On weekends snowmobiles also improve the snow base with hard-packed trails which provide ski tourers with fast paths for the downhill trip. The skier with good endurance may want to continue the easy tour east to the Buckhorn Ranger Station which doubles the tour length. A fast-dropping logging road down the drainage provides a challenging return route for the advanced tourer.

Drive on Colorado 14 west of Ft. Collins to the junction with the Pingree Park Road above Kelly Flats Campground. Turn left onto a large bridge over the Cache la Poudre River and proceed 4.2 miles to the Crown Point Road junction. Fork south and follow the Pingree Park Road another 7.7 miles to the Pennock Pass Road marked by a Buckhorn Ranger Station sign. Private developers often plow the Pingree Park Road but access may be limited by varying local snow conditions. Park on the side of the road.

Begin skiing east on the Pennock Pass Road and immediately cross the bridge over Pennock Creek. Glide through an open area, staying north of a branch creek; pass over a cattle guard and continue the easy climb to a switchback across the creek. An old logging road forks east at the switchback, continuing a parallel course along the branch creek. This smaller, more secluded road makes a delightful alternate route for either the trip in or the return trip.

On the Pennock Pass Road climb gradually west above the creek drainage, then make a wide contour through climax lodgepole pine and continue on the road east and northeast. Turn north across another branch creek and make the steady climb through a series of switchbacks. Soon an opening in the lodgepole pine reveals a vast panorama of the Mummy Range west and the rocky Stormy Peaks ridgetop southwest. A series of jagged glacial cirques between white, dome-shaped Comanche Peak and Fall Mountain west-southwest highlight the vista.

The open roadbed continues on a gradual, winding climb up the steep south-facing mountainside. From the top of the pass an advanced return route follows a logging road west down the drainage. Stay in the scattered lodgepole pine north of the clear-cut area and drop quickly down the snow-filled roadbed. Continue through pine seedlings, then double pole into thicker aspen and spruce as the roadbed begins to level. Glide north of the willow-filled creekbed on a winding, shaded trail, intersect the Pennock Pass Road at the first switchback, and continue west to the parking area.

Tattooed aspen

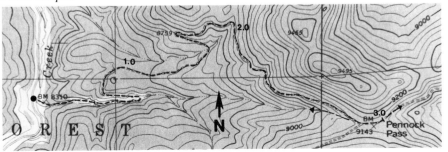

41 PINGREE PARK

One day trip
Classification: Intermediate
Distance: 5.5 miles round trip
Skiing time: 3.5 hours round trip
Elevation gain: 560 feet
Maximum elevation: 9,460 feet
Season: Mid-December through March
Topographic maps:
   U.S.G.S. Pingree Park, Colo. 7.5'

#41 PINGREE PARK

The loop route into Pingree Park, beginning near mile 2.5 of the described trail, crosses property owned by Colorado State University and others and is now closed to the ski touring public. Please observe the posted "No Trespassing" signs and respect this closure! Two additional ski tours within the Poudre Ranger District are the Monument Gulch trail and the Crown Point Saddle trail, both containing good snow conditions during the touring season, adequate trailhead parking, and terrain gentle enough for beginning tourers. For more information, obtain the pamphlet entitled "Winter Backcountry Use Information/Ski Touring and Ski Mountaineering" from the Poudre Ranger District, 148 Remington, Fort Collins, CO 80521.

Sometime in the late 1860's George Pingree, old-time trapper on the Cache la Poudre River, guided lumber contractors for the Union Pacific Railroad to virgin stands of timber along the headwaters of the "Little South." Spurred by the demand for railroad ties, crews of "tie boys" soon followed and lumber camps sprang up along the river. After the tie boom, pioneer Hugh Ramsey homesteaded in Pingree Park and continued lumber operations, ingeniously piping water down the hill from Fall Creek to power his sawmill. From Tom Bennett Campground the tour follows a hilltop route to Fall Creek, descends the hill next to the old pipeline site, and loops through the windy park bottom to Pingree Park Road.

Drive on Colorado 14 to the Pingree Park Road junction above the Kelly Flats Campground. Turn left onto a large bridge over the Cache la Poudre River and proceed 4.2 miles to the Crown Point Road junction. Fork south and continue on the Pingree Park Road toward the Tom Bennett Campground turnoff, another 11.6 miles. In early December the road usually drifts closed just beyond the Pennock Pass Road turnoff (No. 40), adding several more miles to the length of the tour. Park along the side of the road.

Ski over the unplowed Pingree Park Road to the Tom Bennett Campground turnoff, marked by a mileage sign. Turn north onto the shaded jeep road and drop to the flat campground area. Cross the bridge over snowfilled South Fork Poudre River and curve west on a gradual climb to a junction with the road to Hourglass and Comanche Reservoirs, an alternate tour route. On the southern horizon, Sugarloaf Mountain, named after the old, cone-shaped loaf of bulk sugar, joins the snow-capped Stormy Peaks to form an alpine panorama.

Follow the rising and falling trail southwest. Pass through a barbed wire fence and continue straight where a branch road drops south to the park bottom. Climb gradually through a mixed conifer forest and eventually pass another southerly branch road. Glide in and out of the trees on the steep mountainside, then swing left and drop slightly across the Fall Creek drainage. Immediately after the creek crossing turn south onto an obscure branch trail, staying to the right of several large boulders. Leave the creek basin and continue south across the mountainside, weaving around seedling lodgepole pine that have begun to grow on the unused trail. The trail drops steeply for the first several yards, then levels and is easier to see.

Glide south through lodgepole pine and aspen, then follow a switchback northeast and continue the steady descent. After a second switchback the trail heads south and breaks from the trees to a good view of willow-lined South Fork Poudre River. Ski through two more switchbacks to the park bottom and continue past a pile of log slabs and rusted gears and wheels, remnants of an early sawmill. Weave through the smooth snow patches that cover the ponds, cross a bridge over the South Fork Poudre River, and glide northeast in and out of the trees on the obvious roadcut. Pass beneath unseen ponds at the east end of the park, cross through the gate to the Pingree Park Road, and make the downhill return to the parking area.

Spring day rest stop

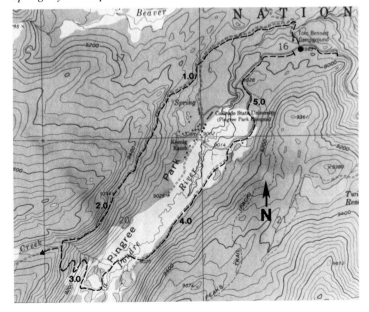

42 CIRQUE MEADOWS

One day trip
Classification: Intermediate
Distance: 3.6 miles one way
Skiing time: 2-2½ hours one way
Elevation gain: 900 feet
Maximum elevation: 9,800 feet
Season: Mid-December through mid-April
Topographic maps:
    U.S.G.S. Pingree Park, Colo. 7.5'
    U.S.G.S. Comanche Peak, Colo. 7.5'

The open clearing at the Fall Creek gaging station, unnamed on the 1962 Comanche Peak topo but known to hikers and ski tourers as "Cirque Meadows," permits a magnificent view of the rugged glacial cirques between Comanche Peak and Fall Mountain. From Tom Bennett Campground the gently rolling trail follows a jeep road along the north wall of Pingree Park, then parallels Fall Creek to the wide, often windy meadow.

Drive on Colorado 14 to the Pingree Park Road junction above the Kelly Flats Campground. Turn left onto a large bridge over the Cache la Poudre River and proceed 4.2 miles to the Crown Point Road junction. Fork south and continue on the Pingree Park Road toward the Tom Bennett Campground turnoff, another 11.6 miles. In early December the road usually drifts closed just beyond the Pennock Pass Road turnoff (No. 40), adding several more miles to the length of the tour. Park beside the road.

Follow the unplowed, wind-crusted Pingree Park Road toward Tom Bennett Campground. Pass a southerly branch road to Twin Lakes, ski through a hairpin turn over the Twin Lakes creek drainage, and climb steadily up the steep, east-facing slope. Curve west and continue to the campground turnoff, marked by a mileage sign, then glide north over a smaller, shaded trail through the flat campground area. Cross the bridge over snow-filled South Fork Poudre River and curve west on a gradual climb to a junction with the road to Hourglass and Comanche Reservoirs, an alternate tour route.

Slender-trunked lodgepole pine replace the ponderosa as the rising and falling trail continues southwest. Follow the road through a barbed wire fence, ski underneath a power line, and continue straight where a branch road drops south to the park bottom. Begin a gradual climb through a conifer forest and eventually pass another southerly branch road. The roadbed cuts southwest through thick timber on the steep mountainside, then breaks clear to a view of the flat Pingree Park bottom. Rust-colored willows frame the frozen, wind-scoured ponds and line the South Fork River as it meanders through the valley.

Glide back into the trees on the level road, then swing left and cross Fall Creek. Continue straight where a branch trail forks south to Pingree Park (No. 41) and begin a gradual climb through deep snow on the shaded, north-facing slope. Pass a pile of log slabs from an old sawmill site and proceed through the dense conifer forest, staying right where the Mummy Pass Trail climbs left. Climb more steeply through several switchbacks, veer closer to the Fall Creek drainage north, and break through the trees to a spectacular vista beyond the windy Cirque Meadows. Comanche Peak west, rounded and barren, forms a steep northern wall for the Fall Creek watershed. South of Comanche Peak a series of deep, precipitous cirques fringed with cornices are carved into the Mummy Range. Return over the ski tracks or via the Pingree Park loop.

Beaver spikes

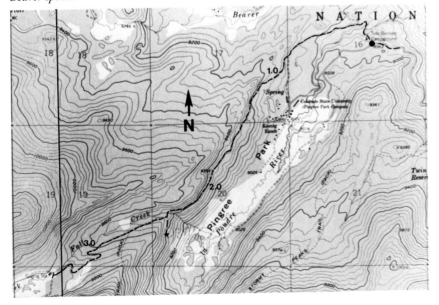

43 BEAVER PARK

One day trip
Classification: Intermediate
Distance: 5.5 miles one way
Skiing time: 2½-3 hours one way
Elevation gain: 1,190 feet
Maximum elevation: 9,330 feet
Season: January through March
Topographic map:
  U.S.G.S. Rustic, Colo. 7.5'

Quiet Beaver Park appears suddenly at the hillside bottom as the trail breaks out of dense lodgepole pine and aspen. A series of frozen beaver ponds, filling the Little Beaver Creek valley, are evidence of an active beaver colony in the park. These deep pools abound with small brook trout.

The last few hundred yards to the bottom of Beaver Park drop sharply; few turnouts on the narrow roadbed increase the difficulty to control speed. Except for this final descent the gradual climb to Beaver Park makes an easy and pleasant tour. The trail beginning can be wind-scoured and although snowmobile use helps keep the trail packed and snow-covered, touring is best after periods of recent snowfall.

Drive on Colorado 14 to the Pingree Park Road junction above the Kelly Flats Campground. Turn left onto a large bridge over the Cache la Poudre River; proceed 6.2 miles to the Flower Road turnoff, forking south where the Crown Point Road continues west. Park off the road near the turnoff.

Begin skiing west on the winding road through an open meadow. Turn gradually southwest and glide through the scattered ponderosa pine and aspen, passing through two barbed wire fences. Double pole down the long hillside and join a branch trail and creekbed near the 1.0 mile mark. Follow the creekbed northwest on a gradual climb through the large meadow. Here rust-colored ponderosa pine, victims of the mountain pine beetle, stand out in stark contrast against the white countryside.

Continue through a grove of aspen to another open meadow, staying right past a snow-swept jeep road to Jacks Gulch. Glide by the fenced watering tank of Bedsprings Springs, and climb gradually into the aspen and ponderosa pine again. Ski north of the willow-filled creekbed in Jacks Gulch meadow and re-enter the trees with a short, steep climb. Follow the road on an easy, rolling climb in and out of the small parks, then shortcut the road west through the last meadow. A sign at the far end of this meadow directs travel to Beaver Park.

Lodgepole pine, replacing the ponderosa, soon hem the road tightly. The tree cover on this shady, north-facing slope holds deep drifts through late spring when bear tracks may sometimes be seen on the crusted snow. Proceed west through the rising and falling terrain, soon beginning the steep descent into Beaver Park. Snowplow the hillside to the park bottom for a closer inspection of the many frozen beaver ponds. The tour can be continued west on the Flowers Trail toward the barren slopes of the Mummy Range. Return via a loop tour down Little Beaver Creek or follow the ski tracks out.

Bear tracks on Flowers Road

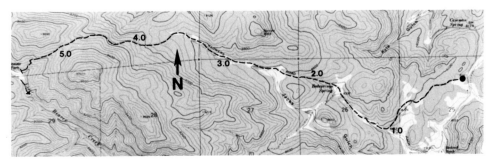

44 SALT CABIN PARK

Half-day trip
Classification: Beginner to Intermediate
Distance: 1.8 miles round trip
Skiing time: 1-1½ hours round trip
Elevation gain: 440 feet
Maximum elevation: 8,620 feet
Season: January through February
Topographic map:
   U.S.G.S. Rustic, Colo. 7.5'

Due to the lower elevation Salt Cabin Park often serves as a winter haven for deer and elk. They forage for snow-covered grasses on the lower meadowland and lie down during the day in the surrounding aspen groves and ponderosa pine. The opportunity to see wildlife in the park increases by beginning upwind on the east side and touring west through the timber. When not filled with snowmobiles, the open, rolling park bottom makes a vast playground for downhill skiing.

Drive on Colorado 14 to the Pingree Park Road junction above the Kelly Flats Campground. Turn left onto a large bridge over the Cache la Poudre River and proceed 4.2 miles to the Crown Point Road junction. Continue west another 2.6 miles to the open Salt Cabin Park hillside. Access may be limited on the unplowed road by local varying snow conditions. Park along the roadside.

Begin skiing up the east side of the large park. Follow the snow-filled ruts of a jeep road around a protruding clump of ponderosa pine and swing north past a prominent gravel mound. Double pole to the gully bottom, then leave the road and traverse the hillside east through scattered pine and deer-scarred aspen. Continue cross-country through another small drainage, turn northeast under a rocky outcropping and climb gradually up the hillside. Soon the forested West White Pine Mountain, topped with a small black dot of the lookout tower, can be seen southwest on the horizon.

Glide north to the creekbed and begin a gradual climb up the drainage through tall aspen. As the drainage basin becomes filled with spruce and willows, switchback up the east mountainside. Continue northwest to the hilltop, staying west of a branch drainage. From this spot the white-capped Signal Mountains, named by white pioneers after seeing the

Indians' curious smoke signals rise from the mountaintop, are visible above forested ranges south-southeast. The expansive, bald Mummy Range which begins in Rocky Mountain National Park near Lawn Lake (No. 39) dominates the horizon southwest.

Cross-country west through fallen ponderosa pine; traverse the east-facing slope above an aspen grove and eventually intercept the jeep road. Follow the road west on a short but steep climb and continue cross-country under a rocky, snow-barren ridgetop as the road ends. Contour to the next ridge, curve southwest, and drop quickly through the aspen groves toward the park bottom. A few sweeping telemark turns down the smooth, treeless hillside provide the perfect end to the tour.

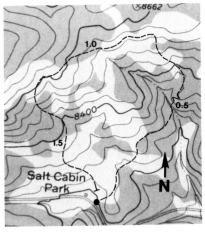

45 PROSPECT MOUNTAIN

Half-day trip
Classification: Intermediate
Distance: 1.5 miles one way
Skiing time: 1 hour one way
Elevation gain: 455 feet
Maximum elevation: 9,135 feet
Season: January through March
Topographic map:
   U.S.G.S. Rustic, Colo. 7.5'

As the crow flies, Prospect Mountain measures little more than one mile from the Colorado 14 highway yet it usually remains isolated from winter visitors. Deer hunters in late fall are the last to tramp the mountainside before drifting snow on the Crown Point Road makes access difficult. For ski tourers, however, the trailhead can be reached by skiing an additional one or two miles up the wide road. If the extension proves too long, stop at the more accessible Salt Cabin Park (No. 44).

After a short climb the Prospect Mountain trail drops gently to Mineral Springs Gulch, then resumes the climb to a mine digging just below the summit. A short scramble to the rocky mountaintop provides a bird's-eye view of the deep Cache la Poudre River valley and the mountain village of Rustic. The valley opens northeast to white snow-patches of Indian Meadows. Farther north Prohibition Mountain rises above the forested ranges and twenty miles west the snow-capped peaks of the Medicine Bow Range glisten on the horizon.

Drive on Colorado 14 to the Pingree Park Road junction above the Kelly Flats Campground. Turn left onto a large bridge over the Cache la Poudre River and proceed 4.2 miles to the Crown Point Road. Continue west on the road another 6.8 miles to the Prospect Mountain trailhead, a narrow roadcut on the mountainside north of the Crown Point Road. Park off the side of the road.

Ski northeast up the roadcut passing a sign which indicates the mileage to Prospect Mountain at an exaggerated 3.0 miles. Pass a small mine pit at the hilltop, curve northwest, and double pole down the hillside through a stand of lodgepole pine. In spring the exposed first section of the trail can be rocky but snow conditions improve considerably once in the trees.

Turn west through an aspen grove and continue the gradual descent into Mineral Springs Gulch. Ski through the willows near the creekbed and turn up the drainage, passing an alternate tour route which heads down the drainage. Follow the road into another meadow, climbing gradually through big aspen trees and stately blue spruce. Re-enter the lodgepole pine at the west end of the meadow; turn north and begin the gradual climb up Prospect Mountain. Cross through a bark-scarred aspen grove, break from the trees, and continue to the end of the road south. Leave skis and hike through the scattered limber pine and scrubby aspen to the mountaintop vista. Return over the ski tracks.

Brush in Mineral Springs Gulch

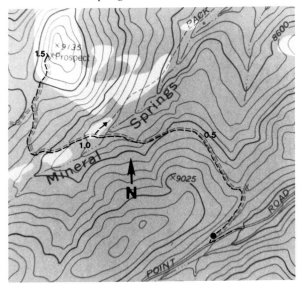

46 BIG SOUTH TRAIL

One day trip or overnight
Classification: Intermediate to Advanced
Distance: 6.8 miles one way
Skiing time: 4-4½ hours one way
Elevation gain: 1,060 feet
Maximum elevation: 9,500 feet
Season: Mid-December through mid-April
Topographic maps:
  U.S.G.S. Boston Peak, Colo. 7.5'
  U.S.G.S. Chambers Lake, Colo. 7.5'

From the Big South Campground on Colorado 14, the Big South Trail follows the Cache la Poudre River into Rocky Mountain National Park. The river's unique name derives from early fur traders in Colorado, French-speaking Creoles from St. Louis. A sudden snowstorm in early fall of 1836 forced a party of these mountain men to abandon their camp, near present-day Bellevue, for a milder climate. They hurriedly buried supplies, black powder and all, along the riverbank and returned the next spring, finding their precious treasure undisturbed. Henceforth they always spoke of the river as the hiding place for powder: La Cache la Poudre.

Both the less protected, more scenic Big South Trail and the wider, easier Cache la Poudre riverbed present excellent tour routes. The trail winds up and down the steep mountainsides for four miles, then continues across a wider valley floor to a footbridge. In this flat terrain thick conifers provide shelter for an overnight camping spot. From the footbridge the tourer can continue many more miles up the riverbed or climb west to Peterson Lake and return down Long Draw Road and Colorado 14 (No. 48).

Drive on Colorado 14 toward the Big South Campground several miles below Chambers Lake. Stop before crossing the bridge near the campground, staying on the east side of the Cache la Poudre River. Park along the wide east shoulder of the highway.

From the parking area ski south past several initial-carved aspens and immediately come to a sign with summer trail mileages. Begin climbing the hillside beyond the sign, staying above a wide roadcut that extends to the river. Herringbone a steep section, then wind southeast on the narrow trail under a rocky hillside. Soon double pole close to the riverbed and glide in and out of deep shadows from the englemann spruce. After another climb and descent break into an open meadow near the 1.0 mile mark. Here the valley floor widens slightly and thick willows line either side of the trail.

Curve away from the river and glide through deep snow in a forest of mixed conifers and aspens. Climb higher on the mountainside and swing east through a boulder field. On the high, rugged ridgetop above the trail, twisted limber pine make black silhouettes against the sky; far below the trail, black water-cuts in the white riverbed create more contrasting patterns. Bend south into the trees again, pass through a shallow gully, and glide over the snowy footbridge across May Creek. Drop and rise through another drainage, then ski past a precipitous mountainside west. Double pole to the riverbed, then begin a steep climb southwest. On the west side of the river, two forested mountains form a riflesight view of white, barren Clark Peak nearly seven miles away.

Follow the narrow, winding path high up the mountainside, then begin a long, smooth descent. Glide through sheltering fir and lodgepole pine on a rolling trail, leaving then returning to the riverbed. Ski cross-country near the river as the trail becomes confusing. Eventually turn east, climb slightly through small aspens, and continue a southeast course to a wooden footbridge across the river. Ideal overnight campsites, protected by thick conifers and willows, can be found throughout this section. Return down the riverbed or on a longer loop tour via Long Draw Road and Colorado 14.

Spring skiing on Big South Trail

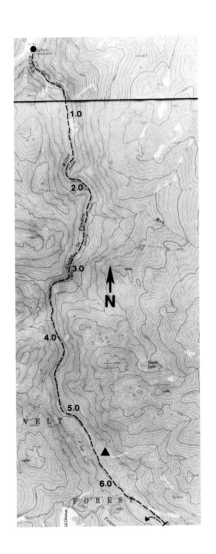

47 BARNES MEADOW RESERVOIR

Half-day trip
Classification: Beginner
Distance: 2.1 miles one way
Skiing time: 1-1½ hours one way
Elevation gain: 260 feet
Maximum elevation: 9,250 feet
Season: Mid-December through April
Topographic map:
   U.S.G.S. Chambers Lake, Colo. 7.5′

The small creek basin east of Barnes Meadow Reservoir lies hidden between forested mountainsides but the delightful cross-country tour up the drainage should not be overlooked. The tour route follows a sheltered jeep road around the reservoir but with good weather the flat, snow-filled reservoir itself allows oppportunity for smooth, unobstructed gliding. An unpromising beginning of dense forest in the creek basin, too constricted for snowmobiles, soon loosens enough for a winding, secluded trail. A small knoll immediately south of the high point on the trail overlooks the deep Cache la Poudre River valley and provides a particularly inviting spot for lunch and relaxation.

Drive toward the Chambers Lake area west of Ft. Collins on Colorado 14; proceed past the Big South Campground onto the dirt road and continue as far as road conditions permit, usually near the junction with the Laramie River Road. Park off the road, making sure not to block the access of other cars.

Begin skiing south on Colorado 14, following east of the large Joe Wright Creek drainage. Pass a very long, dilapidated lodginghouse and another old log cabin on the east side of the road and continue south on the wide road. As soon as the white banks of Barnes Meadow Reservoir spillway are visible down the road, turn east onto a jeep road; cross through a barbed wire fence and glide through the lodgepole pine. Pass an aspen grove where deer have scarred the bark and double pole down the hillside to the east end of the reservoir.

Glide east through a wide meadow to the creek basin and pass through a flat area of dead, standing aspen. Where dense conifers from the mountainside spill into the drainage, stay close to the creekbed on a cross-country route. Pass through a small park filled with willows and continue on a winding path through giant fir trees and tall aspen. Black claw marks on several aspen trees show where bears have climbed the trees.

Continue through a glen of small aspen and turn south out of the drainage bottom as the mountainside begins to drop. Switchback up a small knoll to a superb vantage point and lunch spot. Three rolling, forested mountain peaks above the Cache la Poudre River comprise the panorama east. Return over the ski tracks.

Spring skiing near Barnes Meadow Reservoir

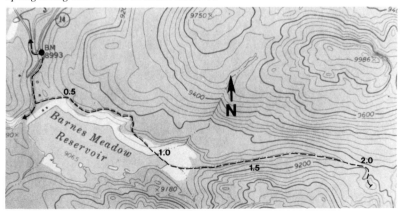

48 JOE WRIGHT RESERVOIR

One day trip
Classification: Intermediate
Distance: 5.2 miles one way
Skiing time: 3½-4 hours one way
Elevation gain: 910 feet
Maximum elevation: 9,900 feet
Season: December through April
Topographic map:
   U.S.G.S. Chambers Lake, Colo. 7.5'

When snowplows begin to open Cameron Pass in April, six feet of snow may still cover the Colorado 14 roadbed, indicative of the long skiing season in this area. Except for a shortcut across the open, sometimes windy Chambers Lake, the tour follows this wide, rolling roadbed all the way to Joe Wright Reservoir. With provisions for an overnight the tour can be continued several more miles to the top of Cameron Pass. A return trip down the more

secluded Joe Wright creekbed adds variety to the tour and eliminates competition with any snowmobile traffic. The Long Draw Road to the Big South Trail via Peterson Lake presents another excellent alternate route for a long day trip or overnight (See No. 46).

Drive toward the Chambers Lake area on Colorado 14. Proceed past the Big South Campground onto the dirt road and continue as far as road conditions permit, usually near the junction with the Laramie River Road. Park off the side of the road, making sure not to block the access of other cars.

Begin skiing south on the Colorado 14 roadbed; curve southwest near the Barnes Meadow Reservoir dam and glide through the lodgepole pine forest toward Chambers Lake. Leave the road as it swings around the lake shore and double pole onto the large lakebed. Curve south into the Trap Creek inlet and follow the west shoreline to Chambers Lake Campground. Cross-country south through the trees from the campground; cross an access road to the boat ramp and pass a bulletin board with topographic maps.

Rejoin the Colorado 14 roadbed and proceed on a gradual climb through a series of switchbacks. Follow the winding road, staying east of the Joe Wright Creek basin and continue southwest as the steeper Long Draw Road forks south to Peterson Lake. Cross the bridge over Joe Wright Creek and glide next to the creekbed which soon winds out of tree cover and continues through a snowy basin. Turn south off the roadbed as the basin meadow widens, cross North Fork Creek, and climb cross-country through a switchback to the roadbed. Soon the dense lodgepole pine along the road funnel vision toward flat-topped Bald Mountain southeast.

Follow the roadbed on a gradual climb out of the trees to the deep, empty Joe Wright Reservoir bowl. From the north end of the reservoir a wide panorama of white peaks is visible beyond densely forested mountainsides. Bald Mountain and an unnamed long range lie east, the Never Summer Mountains jut prominently south, and the southernmost extension of the Medicine Bow Mountains can be seen west. For an alternate return route ski down the uncluttered Joe Wright creekbed. Avoid the dangerously steep wash below the Joe Wright Reservoir spillway, climb around the bridges that are too constricted to ski under, and follow the creekbed to Chambers Lake. Cross to the east end of the lake and continue over the ski tracks to the parking area.

Snow-filled footbridge

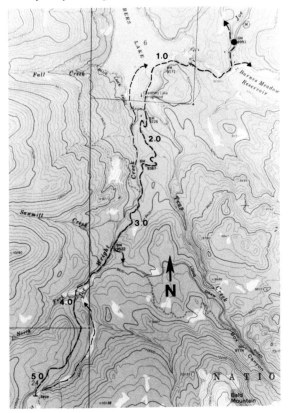

49 GREEN RIDGE TRAIL

One day trip
Classification: Beginner to Advanced
Distance: 4.2 miles one way
Skiing time: 3-3½ hours one way
Elevation gain: 500 feet
Maximum elevation: 9,490 feet
Season: Mid-December through April
Topographic maps:
  U.S.G.S. Chambers Lake, Colo. 7.5'
  U.S.G.S. Boston Peak, Colo. 7.5'

From the trailhead near Lost Lake the Green Ridge Trail follows a winding course between the Cache la Poudre River valley east and the Laramie River valley west, eventually ending a few miles south of Deadman Park (No. 51). Immediate stopping places for the flat, easy-gliding tour include Lost Lake, Laramie Lake, and west Twin Lake. On weekends snow-mobilers claim the Laramie River Road as their own but usually stay out of the deeper snow on the Green Ridge Trail.

Drive toward the Chambers Lake area on Colorado 14; proceed past the Big South Campground onto the dirt road and continue to the Laramie River Road junction or as far as road conditions permit. Occasionally the Laramie River Road is plowed past the Green Ridge Trailhead. Park on the side of the road, making sure not to block the access of other cars.

Begin skiing west on the Laramie River Road. Immediately cross the large bridge over Joe Wright Creek, then climb gradually on the wide roadbed through lodgepole pine. Pass right of a meadow with scattered aspens and willows and proceed through a long curve toward Chambers Lake southwest. As the road swings near the east thumb of the lake, a break in the trees reveals south the barren, rounded Bald Mountain and the white, flat-topped range that protrudes from the Never Summer Mountains. Climb steadily through thick lodgepole pine near the northeast side of Chambers Lake, then curve north and continue toward the snowy Lost Lake bowl.

Immediately before the Laramie River Road curves west and drops, turn north onto the Green Ridge Trail, marked by a sign with summer trail mileages. Ski northwest through a wide cut in the lodgepole pine to a half-buried picnic table and turn right onto a narrow, red-flagged trail. Glide above the west side of Lost Lake, maintaining elevation where branch trails drop east to the lakebed. Soon glide gently downhill, following the middle trail as a left fork, marked with blue flags, climbs uphill and a right fork drops more steeply toward Lost Lake. Curve east, pass a sign that indicates 0.5 mile to Laramie Lake, and double pole to a creek basin. Leave the summer trail and ski cross-country up the drainage, staying close to the creekbed. Break into a long meadow and continue west to Laramie Lake. Along the north end of the large lake the tourer can find pine-sheltered lunch spots with a grand view south of Bald Mountain and a flat-topped range.

Rejoin the Green Ridge Trail in the open area immediately north of Laramie Lake and continue north through a stand of lodgepole pine. Ski into a large meadow where a branch trail forks northeast to east Twin Lake. Cross to the northwest end of the meadow, glide in and out of lodgepole pine and aspens to a flat, north-south meadow, and proceed north to the west Twin Lake bowl. Return over the ski tracks.

Green Ridge Trail

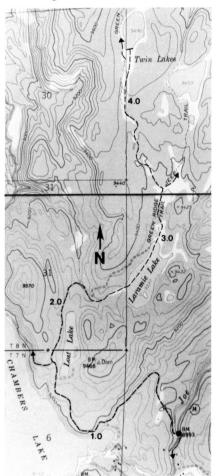

50 OLD BALLARD ROAD

One day trip
Classification: Beginner to Intermediate
Distance: 2.8 miles one way
Skiing time: 1½-2 hours one way
Elevation gain: 885 feet
Maximum elevation: 8,880 feet
Season: January through February
Topographic map:
  U.S.G.S. Crystal Mountain, Colo. 7.5'

A tour on Old Ballard Road never seems steep at any one spot but the gradual climb results in a surprising elevation gain of almost 900 feet for the short 2.8 miles. The return trip is easy but fast, especially if snowmobiles have packed the snow. For excellent information on snow conditions and additional trails consult the snow ranger at nearby Buckhorn Ranger Station.

Drive to the Buckhorn Canyon Road either west from Horsetooth Reservoir through Ma-sonville or through Rist Canyon and the Stove Prairie Cutoff Road. From the Stove Prairie/Buckhorn Canyon Road junction proceed west another 10.3 miles where a sign on the north side of the road marks the beginning of the Old Ballard Logging Road. Park off the road.

Begin skiing southeast on the unplowed roadbed, immediately crossing Buckhorn Creek. Follow east of the willow-covered Cascade Creek and soon glide through a meadow area. Continue a gradual climb past a private gate on the left, cross Cascade Creek, and switchback north. Young, black-barked lodgepole pine line both sides on the wide roadbed through another switchback, then give way for a grand vista of the forested Cascade Creek valley. A high, rocky bluff distinguishes Lookout Mountain south from the other rolling, forested hills.

Continue back into the lodgepole pine and aspen, staying on the middle road as side roads branch off from either side. Switchback north, then veer left as the Greer road forks right. Pass through an aspen grove and climb steadily up the east-facing slope. The road proceeds through a series of three more switchbacks to the mountaintop, passing and re-passing the steeper Donner Hill Trail.

Leave the Ballard Road a few yards before it begins the first drop; ski west on a branch road through an aspen grove to a small quartz outcropping. Cache skis here and hike northwest another hundred yards over the hill-crest to a good view point and secluded lunch spot. The lookout tower on West White Pine Mountain due north appears as a black dot on the horizon and wide Monument Gulch northwest can easily be identified. The Buckhorn Creek valley west opens to a flat park and a dark line under the rolling crest of the far mountainside delineates an area logged in the 1940's.

The tour can be continued several more miles on the Old Ballard Road as it drops into the Buckhorn Creek valley, then winds up the mountainside west. The return trip over the ski tracks descends with sufficient grade for long, easy gliding and an occasional jump from the snow-drifted waterbars in the road adds more excitement.

114

Downhill run

51 DEADMAN PARK

Overnight
Classification: Advanced
Distance: 11.5 miles one way
Skiing time: 5-5½ hours one way
Elevation gain: 1,630 feet
Maximum elevation: 10,270 feet
Season: December through April
Topographic maps:
    U.S.G.S. South Bald Mountain, Colo. 7.5'
    U.S.G.S. Deadman, Colo. 7.5'

The macabre name of "Deadman Creek" shows on the earliest maps of Colorado National Forest, now called Roosevelt National Forest; later the name appears on other features: Deadman Park, Deadman Hill, and Deadman Road. Perhaps the name spread through the area because the original incident was tragic and haunting. Old-timers in Red Feather Lakes Village tell this story: on a lonely wintertime "trap run" a mountain man came upon a bear carcass in his trap near Deadman Hill. He tied up his horse and removed the carcass from the trap. As he attempted to reset the trap, the steel jaws slipped from his grip and snapped shut on his arm. There he lay beside a bear carcass and tethered horse, struggling to free himself; there three sun-bleached skeletons were found in the following summer—with a rusted bear trap still locked tightly onto an arm bone.

Although few ski tourers have seen Deadman Park in winter, this vast and trackless territory holds unlimited tour possibilities. Logging roads branch in every direction across clear-cut slopes. Willow-filled meadows lead into uncluttered creekbeds. Narrow jeep trails tunnel through thickly-forested mountainsides. The 1967 Deadman topo, up-to-date except around Nunn Creek Basin where there have been recent logging operations, is an essential aid in sorting out these routes. Unlike the steep climbs and shussbooming returns that characterize many of the tours farther south, the terrain here rises and falls gently, giving an ideal combination of long glides and easy climbs to the tours. The one-way distance from snow closure on Deadman Road to Deadman Park measures about 11.5 miles, usually too long for an out-and-return trip. An overnight camp in Deadman Park, however, allows a relaxed pace for the tour and serves as a centralized base for half-day trips to Deadman Lookout Tower (No. 52), the Sand Creek area, and Nunn Creek Basin.

From Fort Collins drive on U.S. 287 to The Forks; turn west onto the Livermore Road and proceed toward the Red Feather Lake area. Drive west where roads fork north to Red Feather Lakes Village; join Deadman Road and continue as far as road conditions permit, usually another two miles. Occasionally a logging company keeps the road open through December. Park off the side of the road.

Begin skiing west and northwest on Deadman Road. Climb through crusted snow drifts near the starting point and glide in and out of

Spring camping

several flat, wind-swept meadows. In the first mile the road tends to be wind-scoured in winter and bare of snow in spots in spring. But conditions improve steadily as more and more ponderosa pine line the road. Look for the snowy summit of Middle Bald Mountain which shows briefly on the distant skyline southwest, then disappears behind a long, forested range. Cross North Lone Pine Creek and follow the winding road north, soon gaining an expansive viewpoint of the level plains and forested hills around Red Feather Lakes. Continue through four switchbacks on an easy climb up the east-facing mountainside. Pass an old logging area which is visible through the trees south, then turn northwest and ski over the crest of the hillside.

Glides soon become longer and easier as the roadbed drops gently through a bend southwest, crosses a small tributary of the North Fork Poudre River, and swings northwest again. Pass a logging road which heads south and continue the easy descent, turning south through a more open area of scattered limber pine, then crossing a small drainage. Glide west to another tributary of the North Fork Poudre River, climb slightly northwest, and pass a re-forested area of seedling lodgepole pine. The trees change to a thick, mature stand as the road turns west-southwest and drops gradually to the bridge over Killpecker Creek. Ski south of the North Fork Poudre Campground, climb gradually to a crossing over the North Fork, and proceed west past another good tour route that switchbacks northeast.

The road winds west through the North Fork valley, crosses a small drainage, and climbs gradually southwest. Ski through another drainage and contour around the mountainside to a westerly direction again. Soon snow-filled meadows along the riverbed are visible through the trees as the road continues on a gradual, winding climb. Proceed through a switchback east, then bend north on a slightly steeper climb up the hillside. Pass an easterly logging road, switchback south, and continue the climb to a good viewpoint of white, clear-cut slopes surrounding Nunn Creek Basin south. Thick lodgepole pine soon block this view as the snow-filled road winds northwest and eventually passes north of a large meadow.

Glide west through the lodgepole pine to a sign which reads: "Deadman Hill/Elevation 10,270 feet." Here a branch road leads south through the trees, providing access to the beautiful but challenging Green Ridge Trail. The road crosses several miles of windy, clear-cut slopes, angles west to a branch of Nunn Creek, and stays with this creekbed through Nunn Creek Basin to an intersection with the Green Ridge Trail south. After crossing the vast expanse of Green Ridge, the trail passes Emerald Lake, heads south to east Twin Lake, and continues as described in Green Ridge Trail (No. 49). This tour of more than 25 miles requires a minimum of two overnight camps and demands well-practiced orientation and winter camping skills.

Proceed west along the top of Deadman Hill; keep straight where a branch road drops to an east extension of Deadman Park and pass the northerly Deadman Fire Lookout Road. Break trail on the snowy road and soon begin a gentle, steady descent through the lodgepole pine and englemann spruce forest. Swing north to a willow-filled creekbed, pass a southerly branch road, and gradually break from the trees to open snow fields of Deadman Park. Leave the road south, cross through a drifted buck fence, and ski cross-country through the long park. In the sheltering trees around the park, the tourer can find an ideal overnight camping spot, perhaps with a view of the distant, snow-capped peaks in the Rawah Wilderness Area southwest.

For an alternate return to Deadman Road, ski cross-country into the east extension of Deadman Park. Dip through a creek basin and follow the treeline until intercepting an east-west roadcut. Follow the road as it continues east; stay above the willows in the park bottom, then cross through another creek basin below a collapsed, snow-drifted bridge. After winding south and east through a third drainage, the road gradually re-enters the lodgepole pine, bends northeast, and begins a gradual climb. Break trail up the winding roadcut to an intersection with Deadman Road and return over the ski tracks. Ski down the creekbed south of the road for a faster descent down Deadman Hill.

118

Rare glimpse of Rocky Mountain Bighorn Sheep

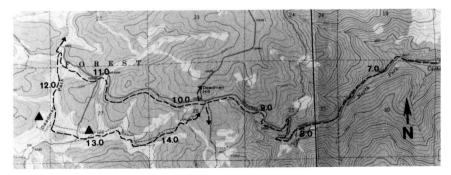

52 DEADMAN LOOKOUT TOWER

One day trip or overnight
Classification: Advanced
Distance: 2.5 miles one way (from Deadman Hill)
Skiing time: 1-1½ hours one way
Elevation gain: 440 feet
Maximum elevation: 10,710 feet
Season: December through April
Topographic map:
  U.S.G.S. Deadman, Colo. 7.5′

Thick stands of lodgepole pine block any vista along the snowy Deadman Fire Lookout Road until the final few hundred yards to the windy tower hilltop. Then the view increases dramatically to a beautiful panorama that includes the Wyoming plains north and Rocky Mountain National Park south. By mid-December drifting snow closes the Deadman Road about two miles west of the Red Feather Lakes turnoff and brings the total one way distance of the tour to about 12.5 miles. Even with fast snow only strong skiers will be able to make the tour in one day. Others will want to enjoy a more leisurely pace by camping in the sheltering trees around North Fork Poudre Campground or near the open Deadman Park. In

April the tourer may have to hike over a few patches of bare ground after parking at the snow drifts but pleasant spring skiing conditions compensate for this bother: a sun-hardened snow crust facilitates faster, effortless gliding; generally warmer weather makes better camping conditions; and the tour route has less snowmobile traffic.

From Fort Collins drive on U.S. 287 to The Forks. Turn west onto the Livermore Road and proceed toward the Red Feather Lakes area. Drive west where roads fork north to Red Feather Lakes Village. Join Deadman Road and continue as far as road conditions permit, usually another two miles. Park off the side of the road.

Begin skiing west on the Deadman Road and eventually descend to the North Fork Poudre Campground. Continue next to the North Fork Cache la Poudre River to the top of Deadman Hill. For a complete description of this part of the tour see Deadman Park (No. 51). Pass a southerly branch road and a sign reading "Deadman Hill/Elevation 10,270 feet." Continue west where another road heads south and turn north a few yards beyond onto the Deadman Fire Lookout Road. The wide road cuts through thick lodgepole pine and englemann spruce on an easy climb toward the top of Deadman Hill, then angles northeast and becomes more level. Soon turn north and glide over the smooth snow lane through a black-trunked pine forest. This dense timber blocks the view on either side of the road, channeling vision south to the clear-cut slopes near Nunn Creek Basin.

Continue north over the sheltered roadbed, then curve gradually east. Occasional englemann spruce appear among the lodgepole pine as the rising and falling road swings north again. Begin an easy, steady climb and soon break into the open meadow southwest of the Deadman Lookout Tower. Ski northwest, short-cutting the road, then hike the last few hundred feet across a snowbare hillside to the base of the tower. A locked chain fence prevents access to the lookout top but the 360° panoramic view remains undiminished. With clear weather a sharp eye can pick out Laramie north-northeast and Cheyene east-northeast on the hazy Wyoming plains. Several rocky peaks dominate the view of Rawah Wilderness area southwest and a sea of deep blue hills leads to the long, white Mummy Range in Rocky Mountain National Park on the distant horizon south. The return trip over a broken trail takes only half the time as the trip in.

Deadman Lookout Tower

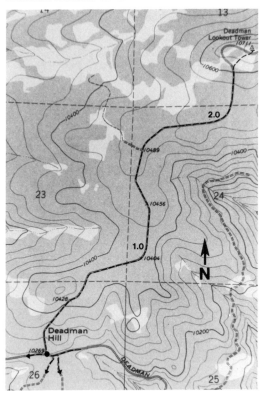

53 BEAR CREEK

One day trip
Classification: Beginner
Distance: 5.8 miles round trip
Skiing time: 3½-4 hours round trip
Elevation gain: 160 feet
Maximum elevation: 9,040 feet
Season: Mid-December through April
Topographic map:
  U.S.G.S. Woods Landing, Wyo. 7.5'

From Laramie, drive on Wyoming 230 through Woods Landing to the Chimney Park Boy Scout Camp. Proceed past the east entrance to the camp and park off the road near the beginning of the barricaded west entrance.

Ski west several yards on the highway shoulder, passing a long snow fence north of the road. Turn south into an open meadow and glide across the flat terrain, soon curving west over a branch of Woods Creek. Ski to the west end of the meadow, swing south into the lodgepole pine on a small roadcut and continue to the intersection of a wide east-west road. Occasionally the white snow patch around Chimney Park Lake can be seen from the trail but usually thick stands of pine, many marked with blue dye for timbering, block the view of any distant landmark.

Proceed west about fifty yards and turn left onto a smaller jeep road. Glide south through deep snow on the level roadbed, eventually breaking from the trees into an old clear-cut area. Immediately southeast a windy, barren knoll, distinguished with several dead standing tree trunks, protrudes above the level forest floor. Ski through the clear-cut area, pass a branch road that drops southwest, and contour east to the south side of the knoll. Soon the mountainside south of Bear Creek can be seen from the trail, the dense pine cover interrupted only by a prominent aspen grove.

Pick a cross-country route toward the aspen grove and double pole the hillside to Bear Creek. Cross through the creek basin and over a wide road which parallels the drainage, ski south through a small meadow, and begin climbing on the east side of the aspen grove. A panorama of rolling, forested mountains comes to view west as the road climbs gradually south and southwest. Keep right where a road joins at a diagonal, continue across near-level terrain, and intersect another east-west road. Turn left and proceed into a thick forest area, passing several southerly logging roads. Leave the climax forest and eventually ski through an old clear-cut section now covered with pine seedlings. A scenic view of the rugged, snow-capped Medicine Bow Range on the distant horizon southeast makes this open area a pleasant lunch spot.

Continue east on the roadbed, re-enter the tall lodgepole pine, and begin descending the north-facing slope. As the road levels, turn north at a crossroads and drop to Bear Creek. Ski west up the creek basin, closing the tour loop near the aspen grove, and retrace the ski tracks north to the parking area.

Snow falls early in the pine forest around Chimney Park and still covers the numerous logging roads in spring, giving the area a reputation for excellent, dependable touring conditions. On early morning tours during spring the hardened snow crust permits effortless gliding. But with warm afternoon sun the melting snow gives way with each stride.

Beaver cut stumps

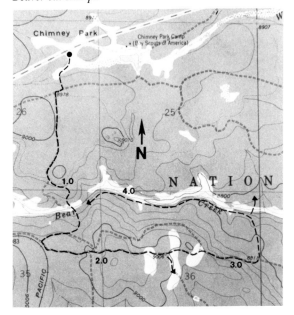

54 CHIMNEY PARK

One day trip
Classification: Beginner
Distance: 7.1 miles round trip
Skiing time: 3½-4 hours round trip
Elevation gain: 300 feet
Maximum elevation: 8,980 feet
Season: Mid-December through mid-April
Topographic map:
  U.S.G.S. Woods Landing, Wyo. 7.5'

The whine of cars along the Wyoming 230 highway penetrates the woods for the first mile of the Chimney Park loop tour but soon only sounds of muffled wind and sibilant ski glides break the silence. The flat, fast route is marked with red spots of paint for most of its length. Except for a short, open area at the east end of the loop, deep snow remains on the shaded trail through April, allowing excellent early morning touring.

From Laramie drive on Wyoming 230 through Woods Landing to the Chimney Park Boy Scout Camp. Proceed past the east entrance to the camp and park off the road near the beginning of the barricaded west entrance.

Begin skiing west along the highway shoulder; pass a long snow fence north of the road and turn south into an open meadow. Curve west over the flat terrain to the end of the meadow, then follow a small roadcut south through the lodgepole pine to a wide east-west road. Glide east over the road, angle right where a power line right-of-way branches left, and continue past an old, half-buried Jelm sign and several handmade Boy Scout campsite signs. Soon spots of red paint appear on trees along the south side of the road, marking the route for the continuation of the tour.

Follow the red markers past two branch roads that fork right then left and continue beyond an aspen grove south of the road. Glide over slightly rolling terrain through thick lodgepole pine; eventually break into an area of young seedlings which permit a glimpse south to distant, timbered slopes, then follow the road southwest through thick timber again. Lodgepole pine give way to aspen and scattered douglas fir as the road curves west, passes a scrubby marsh, and follows north of the wide, snow-filled Jelm Creek drainage, an alternate tour route.

Pass through a barbed wire fence, follow the road across an aspen-and-willow-filled tributary creek, and angle closer to the Jelm Creek drainage south. Ski through an area of beaver-cut aspen trunks and continue west across an open hillside. Soon flat-topped mountains can be seen beyond the Laramie River valley east. Switchback north shortly after this eastern panorama comes into view, then climb the east side of a wide gulley and proceed north-northwest past two easterly branch roads. From the hilltop vantage point snow-capped Medicine Bow Range appears south on the distant horizon above a sea of forested hills.

Re-enter the dense lodgepole pine forest and gradually curve west on the sheltered trail. Continue west where branch trails fork north, pass a meadow visible through the trees south, and eventually ski by several signs that mark the Camp's rifle range. Glide west over the level roadbed, closing the tour loop, and retrace the ski tracks to the parking area.

Rotten snow on late spring tour

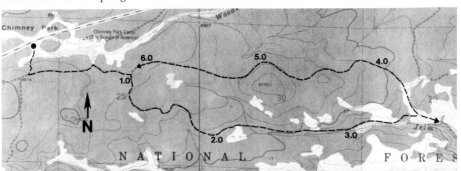

GLOSSARY

ALPINE LIFE ZONE: This zone begins at timberline (about 11,500 feet) and extends to the highest mountain peaks. Low temperatures and high winds create a climate similar to that beyond the Arctic Circle. The wind-packed snowfields cover the grasses, sedges, and dwarf shrubs until late May or June.

AVALANCHE: The "hard slab" avalanche, common along the Front Range, occurs when heavy deposits of wind-drifted snow form on top of unstable bases. The hollow sound of snow drumming or cracking under the skis is one sign of this extremely dangerous condition.

BEARING: The straight line of travel or sight, fixed in relation to the direction north.

BLAZED TRAIL: A trail marked by Forest Service personnel by chipping a small cut above a large cut into the bark of conspicuous trees.

BLUE SPRUCE: A medium-sized tree with stiff, prickly needles, 1-1½ inches long, silvery-blue color; has light brown cones over 3 inches long; generally found below 9,000 feet elevation along creeks or ponds.

BREAK TRAIL: To push through new snow, setting a TRACK for following skiers.

CHINOOK WIND: A warm, dry wind that occasionally descends the Front Range mountains, decreasing the snow cover quickly.

CLEAR-CUTTING: A term used by foresters to describe the logging practice of cutting all the trees on a slope, in contrast to selective cutting.

CONTOUR: To maintain elevation while following the curve of a mountainside.

CROSS-COUNTRY SKIING: As opposed to SKI TOURING, the competitive Nordic sport of racing over a specially prepared TRACK, using light, fragile skis and light boots.

DOUBLE POLE: To achieve forward momentum by planting both ski poles in unison for a propelling push.

DOUGLAS FIR: The common "Christmas tree" with soft, flat needles, 1-1½ inches long, which stick out in all directions from the branch; has cones conspicuous with three-pronged bracts extending beyond scales; found between 8,000 and 9,000 feet.

ENGLEMANN SPRUCE: A tree with prickly needles, 1 inch long; has cones 1-1½ inches long with papery scales; found mostly above 9,000 feet.

FALL LINE: A term used by skiers to describe the angle or course down a mountainside with the fastest drop in elevation.

FLAT TRACK: A prepared TRACK on level terrain where a beginning skier can practice weight shifts, and poling techniques.

FROST-WEDGING: A process of erosion where water runs into rock seams, expands with freezing, and cracks off bits of rock.

GLIDE: To propel oneself forward by sliding one ski at a time, each stride initiated by a "kick" from the weighted ski.

GORP: A high calorie trail snack or emergency food, usually a mixture of nuts, M&Ms, and raisins. Good!

HERRINGBONE: To climb by keeping the ski tips apart, tails together, and ankles turned in, and stepping into the fall line.

HYPOTHERMIA: The gradual lowering of body temperature due to exposure and exhaustion, leading to stupor, collapse, and eventual death.

KLISTER: A very soft wax applied to the ski bottom for icy and slushy snow conditions, usually needed only in the late spring in Colorado.

LIMBER PINE: A soft pine with needles in clusters of five, 1½-3 inches long; becomes twisted and dwarfed in exposed locations; grows in dry, rocky soil, often near timberline.

LODGEPOLE PINE: A hard pine with stiff, dark green needles in clusters of two, 1-3 inches long; has scaly bark of black to light brown color; found between 8,000 and 10,000 feet.

MONTANE LIFE ZONE: This zone lies between 8,000 and 10,000 feet and produces thick forests of lodgepole pine, aspen and spruce. Snow usually remains through the winter on shady north-facing slopes but can melt clear between snowstorms in open meadows and south-facing slopes.

MORAINE: An accumulation of earth and rock debris deposited by a glacier.

PINE TAR: A pine distillate applied to the ski bottom before wax to seal the wood from moisture and to hold the wax better.

PONDEROSA PINE: A hard pine with dark, yellow-green needles in clusters of two or three, 3-7 inches long; has dark bark when young, reddish-orange bark when mature; grows 150 to 180 feet tall.

POWDER SNOW: A fluffy, dry snow that creates ideal skiing conditions, formed with colder temperatures.

SHUSS: To ski quickly downhill with few or no turns; to "downhill."

SIDESTEP: To climb or drop by keeping skis perpendicular to the fall line, moving one ski forward and sideways, then bringing the other ski alongside.

SKI CROSS-COUNTRY: To pick the most logical route where no roads or trails exist.

SKI TOURING: As opposed to CROSS-COUNTRY SKIING, the recreational sport of exploring the "backcountry," using strong, medium-weight skis and higher cut boots; the winter counterpart to summer hiking.

SKI MOUNTAINEERING: The winter sport characterized by steep climbs and long descents, using heavy skis and stiff climbing boots.

SNOW PLOW: To reduce speed or stop by spreading the tails of the skis, bending knees and turning ankles inward to set edges.

SNOWPLOW TURN: To change direction on a down hill run by assuming the SNOW PLOW position and shifting weight to the ski opposite the direction of the turn; used in packed snow or unbreakable crust.

STEP TURN: To change direction on a downhill run by picking up one ski, pointing it in the direction of the turn, shifting weight onto it and bringing the other ski alongside.

SUB-ALPINE FIR: A small tree with soft, flat needles, 1-1½ inches long, crowded toward the upperside of the branch; has purple, erect cones, 2-4 inches long; found at timberline often with englemann spruce. Also called Alpine Fir.

SUB-ALPINE LIFE ZONE: This zone ranges from 10,000 feet to timberline (about 11,500 feet) and contains small, compact tree groups rather than unbroken forests. Dependable snow cover for skiing usually exists here from December through April.

TELEMARK: To provide stability for straight, downhill running over uneven terrain by extending one ski forward, bending both knees, and distributing weight equally between both skis.

TELEMARK TURN: To change direction on a downhill run by assuming a TELEMARK position, then turning the forward ski inward at a steadily widening angle; used in breakable crust and deep snow.

TIMBERBASH: To make a downhill run through thick timber, sometimes on purpose.

TOPO MAP: A graphic representation of part of the earth's surface, showing the location and shape of mountains, valleys, and plains, the network of streams and rivers, and selected manmade features.

TRACK: The parallel path of skis in snow, usually about 8 inches apart; the race course in CROSS-COUNTRY SKIING.

TRAVERSE: To ascend or descend a hill at an angle to the FALL LINE.

WAX: A substance applied to the ski bottom to allow the ski to both glide and grip on the snow.

WEDEL: To link short turns in a rhythmical way.

WHITE FIR: A pale pea-green tree with soft, flat needles, 2-3 inches long; has pale-green to purple, erect cones, 3-5 inches long; found on hillsides with ponderosa pine and douglas fir, and in canyons with blue spruce.

WIND CHILL: The combined cooling power of low temperature, wind, and humidity.

WIND-SCOURED: The condition of an open park, meadow, or road that has been stripped bare of snow by excessive wind.

WHITE-OUT: The loss of depth perception or total loss of visibility during blizzard conditions.

Editor:
Thomas K. Worcester